W9-DBM-854

The Greatest ☆ Skits on Earth

Nappanee United Methodist Youth Group "1989"

THE GREATEST

SKITS

ON EARTH

Wayne Rice and Mike Yaconelli

ZONDERVAN PUBLISHING HOUSE
Grand Rapids, Michigan

THE GREATEST SKITS ON EARTH
Copyright © 1986 by Youth Specialties, Inc.

Youth Specialties Books are published by Zondervan
Publishing House, 1415 Lake Drive, S.E.,
Grand Rapids, Michigan 49506

Library of Congress Cataloging in Publication Data

The greatest skits on earth.
1. Drama in Christian education.   2. Amateur plays.
I. Rice, Wayne.   II. Yaconelli, Mike.   III. Title.
BV1534.4.G74 1986   246'.7   85-26608
ISBN 0-310-35141-3

All rights reserved. No part of this publication may be reproduced, stored
in a retrieval system, or transmitted in any form or by any means—
electronic, mechanical, photocopy, recording, or any other—except for
brief quotations in printed reviews, without the prior permission of the
publisher.

Illustrated by Dan Pegoda
Edited by David Lambert
Designed by Ann Cherryman

Printed in the United States of America

87 88 89 90 91 92 / 12 11 10 9 8 7 6 5

CONTENTS

CHAPTER THREE: Famous Interviews

Some Do
Three Against a Thousand
Will She or Won't She?
You Got Me, Buddy!

Introduction

Every youth worker knows the value of a good skit. There's no better way to win over a group of young people than to make them laugh—and no better way to make them laugh than with a good skit.

A meeting that could be dull and boring without skits can be a fun-filled experience with them. Organizations like Young Life and Campus Life have for many years made skits an important and regular part of their programming for one simple reason: Skits help to attract kids and to make communication with them possible.

Skits get everyone involved. Not only are the participants in the skit involved; so is the audience. And skits help to make (and keep) youth ministry *fun*—even for its leaders. Where else can a grown adult dress up like Little Red Riding Hood, a Sumu wrestler, or Tarzan? What other line of work allows a perfectly sane person to willingly take a pie in the face or to stick his or her head into a bucket of mashed potatoes?

The Greatest Skits on Earth is the biggest and best collection of skits for youth ministry ever published. Some of these skits are classics that have been used successfully for thirty years or more. Others are brand new, appearing in print for the first time. *The Greatest Skits on Earth* includes something for everybody, grouped into seven chapters.

Chapter 1 features short, one-act skits, most of which require a few basic acting skills, like the ability to memorize lines. All of these skits work best with a little rehearsal, a few props or costumes, and participants who are outgoing and have a good sense of humor.

The "slapstick skits" and "sight gags" in chapter two are essentially visual and border on the absurd. Outrageous costumes and actors who are willing to "let it all hang out" make these skits most effective. If you like the Three Stooges, you'll like the skits in chapter 2.

The crazy "interviews" in chapter 3 usually require two participants—the interviewer (the "straight man") and the interviewee (who usually gets all the laughs). Because the humor is almost entirely in the dialogue, it is best to memorize the lines and to *rehearse*.

The "classics" in chapter 4 are more "theatrical"—they require the same kind of preparation as a normal play. There are more actors, sets, and costumes. Of course, most of these skits (like "Rinse the Blood Off My Toga") are spoofs on "real" drama, so you don't have to take them *too* seriously.

Chapter 5 features some of the best (or worst, depending on your point of view) stunts for use with youth groups. Everyone enjoys a good practical joke, and stunts work on the same principle. Somebody usually "gets it." Stunts as skits work best when the "victim" is a leader or someone in the group who is a "good sport," and when the stunts are strictly for fun. Never use stunts to make fun of someone's stupidity. In fact, sometimes it's a good idea to "fix" a stunt so that the victim really "plays along" with the gag just for the benefit of the audience. That way, everyone gets the impression that he or she "fell for it," when actually the whole thing was rigged. Another good idea is to "switch" the stunt, so that the leader who is pulling the stunt on someone else becomes the surprise victim. Most stunts can be switched by doing it a second time and setting it up so that it appears to "backfire" on the leader.

The skits in chapter 6 are all "audience participation" skits. Many of these, like the "Spontaneous Melodramas," require little or no preparation.

In chapter 7, you'll find a collection of "quickie" skits, most of which can best be described as "groaners." They are good precisely because they are so *bad*. They're short, and they're best used to add a touch of comic relief to any program or event. Many of these skits are best when they appear almost "unplanned," like an interruption in the program.

Keep in mind that all of the skits in this book can be adapted to fit your needs or to bring them up to date a year or two from now. There's no rule that says you can't rewrite a script if it will work better for you that way.

Also, remember that these skits can be used for more than mere entertainment. For example, you can use skits for making announcements of coming events—just slip your announcement into the dialogue of the skit. Kids won't forget an announcement when it's presented as part of a good skit.

When choosing skit participants, choose people who are outgoing enough to really have fun during the performance. Don't choose kids who are too shy or inhibited. If your group isn't used to doing skits, have your adult sponsors do a few skits first; it won't be long before the kids in your group will want to try. Acting ability is rarely required. People who participate in skits are not trying to win an Oscar; they are trying to make people laugh. Sometimes the best way to make people laugh is to completely mess up your part, so even a failure in a skit can be a success. Cast boys in girls' roles, girls in boys' roles, big people as little people, and so on.

Costumes for skits should be as ridiculous as possible. If you plan to use skits regularly, visit a thrift shop or second hand store and stock up on some tacky-looking old clothes that you can use for costumes. Old coats, formals, hats, shoes, jewelry and the like come in handy. Start your own "skit closet" and keep adding more costumes and props year after year.

Promote your skits well. Make a big deal out of them. If you are planning to use a skit like "Senior Superman" in chapter 3, put up posters and send out mailers announcing: "THIS WEEK! IN PERSON! THE MAN OF STEEL HIMSELF—SUPER-MAN!" The kids will know that the "real" Superman won't be there, but they will look forward to seeing who or what you come up with as a substitute. If you are doing a skit like "The Midget Skit" in chapter 2, advertise "THE WORLD'S SHORTEST MAN!" Creative publicity and funny skits will generate interest, excitement, and enthusiasm for your youth programs.

One final thought: always use discretion when choosing skits. Some skits are ideal for younger kids; others are better for older youth. Some skits may be funny for some audiences, but in "poor taste" for others. Some skits are too messy for certain indoor settings. You don't want to squirt toothpaste all over somebody's new drapes. Good judgment is always in order.

Most, but not all, of the skits in this book appeared originally in the *Ideas* books, published by Youth Specialties. They were contributed or written by a lot of creative people who definitely know how to recognize a good skit when they see one. We would like to express our sincere thanks to each one of them. At the risk of leaving someone out, their names are listed on the next page:

Paul Albrecht
Jan Augustine
Bill Bellah
Albert Biernesser
Roy Bilyon
Richard Boyd
John Bristow
Ed Clements
David Coppedge
John Coulombe
Cathy Crone
Glenn Davis
Roy J. Delozier
Bob Doggett
Dallas Elder
Dan Engle

Fay Faron
Lawrence Fitzpatrick
Bill Flanagan
Roy Garcia
Jim Green
Ken Harrower
Wes Harty
Chris Herpolsheimer
Keith Herron
Bruce Humbert
Kay Lindskoog
Tom Lowry
Russ Matzke
Tom McKee
Bob & Doug McKenzie
Paul Monsch

John Moyer
John Peters
Bob Phillips
Christine Scott
David Scott
Herb Shipp
Joe Snow
Graham Sowers
John Splinter
Pete Steveson
Ed Stewart
Dave Treat
Vicente Trujillo
Frank Walker
Randy White
Larry Wiens

CHAPTER ONE

SHORT
ONE-ACT
SKITS

ADAM AND EVE

Here's a short skit about our oldest ancestors. They should be dressed, of course, in "fig leaves."

Adam: What a dump. What a dump.
Eve: (*Enters singing.*) Don't sit under the apple tree with anyone else but me. Anyone else but me . . .
Adam: Eve, who else is there to sit under the apple tree with?
Eve: Aw, Adam, can't you take a rib?
Adam: Not like you can. Hey, Eve, what's for supper?
Eve: Water.
Adam: Water? We had water last night. We had water the night before.
Eve: Yeah, but I found a new way to serve it. On the rocks.
Adam: Water, water, that's all we ever have.
Eve: (*crying*) Well, what about me? You never take me anywhere. I have to sit around this stupid rock all day long. All I have to wear is this fig leaf.

Adam: Oh, yeah? You think leaves grow on trees? *(Eve still cries.)* O.K., I'm sorry, Eve, don't cry . . .

Eve: Adam, I'm going to make you a really nice dinner. How would you like a giant marshmallowed meatball?

Adam: Are you able?

Eve: No, Abel's the short one over there. I think maybe you ought to start taking that memory course.

Adam: O.K., let's go out to eat.

Eve: What's out? It hasn't been invented yet. Anyway, we can't go.

Adam: *(naively)* Why not?

Eve: *(flirtingly)* You know why not. . .

Adam: No, I don't. Now, why not?

Eve: *(playfully)* Oh, c'mon, you know why not.

Adam: WHY NOT!

Eve: Cause we gotta stay home and raise Cain.

THE BIG DATE

Bill and Karen have just met each other after being introduced by common friends. This is the first date for both. They have just arrived at a local restaurant for a meal.

Bill: *(embarrassed)* Hi, Karen.

Karen: *(equally embarrassed)* Hi, Bill.

Bill: *(still embarrassed)* Hi, Karen.

Karen: *(still embarrassed)* Hi, Bill.

Bill: Gosh, this is so . . . *(He leaves sentence floating.)*

Karen: Yes, it is so . . . *(She also leaves the sentence floating.)*

Bill: Karen—uh—have you had many dates before?

Karen: The only date I've ever had was on August 13th.

Bill: Oh, really, what was that?

Karen: My birthday. *(Karen then drops her comb on the floor.)*

Bill:	Oh, here! I'll get it. *(As he stoops over, he falls down on the floor.)* I guess I fell for that one, but at least I had a nice trip. *(As Bill stands up, he forgets to pick up the comb.)*
Karen:	Oh, Bill you're so funny! *(suddenly serious)* But would you mind picking up my comb?
Bill:	*(embarrassed)* Oh, yeah, I guess I forgot. *(As Bill squats down, sound effects are heard of his pants ripping. His face registers embarrassment. As he reaches behind him to check out the rip, he falls backward from his squatting position over to his back. At that moment a waiter comes to take the order; not seeing Bill, he trips over him and falls to the floor.)*
Karen:	Oh, my goodness!
Waiter:	*(regaining composure)* What were you doing on the floor, sir? Aren't our seats comfortable enough?
Bill:	Oh, no. The seats are just fine. I was checking to see if the floor was on the level.
Waiter:	*(unbelievingly)* I don't know about the floor, but are *you* on the level? *(Waiter then notices the rip.)* By the way, sir, something terrible has happened to your pants.
Bill:	Yes I know. Isn't that a rip-off? *(Both men stand.)*
Waiter:	Well, would you like me to do anything?
Bill:	Yeah—how about turning your head when I leave?
Waiter:	*(unbelievingly)* Sure thing. . . . Hey, I'll be back in a minute to take your order. *(As waiter leaves, Bill sits back down at the table.)*
Karen:	Bill, I really appreciate your efforts, but my comb is still on the floor.
Bill:	I'm sorry, Karen, but that waiter crushed my ear when he fell on me. What did you say?
Karen:	I said my comb is still on the floor.
Bill:	*(sheepishly)* Your phone is in the store?
Karen:	No! MY COMB IS ON THE FLOOR!
Bill:	*(sheepishly)* Oh! I'm sorry. *(Bends down and gets the comb.)* Well, we may as well order, there's no use in waiting around.
Karen:	I don't mind waiting. Sometimes I even like to wait around.
Bill:	What?
Karen:	I said, it gives me a lift sometimes to wait.
Bill:	Yeah. I like weight lifting too.

Karen: Oh, good grief. Not to change the subject, but what did you do today?

Bill: I got things all straightened out.

Karen: What do you mean?

Bill: I mean I did my ironing. Aren't you *impressed*?

Karen: Not really. I did my laundry today, too.

Bill: I *knew* I smelled bleach! But I thought it was just your hair.

Karen: *(offended)* Well, I never . . .

Bill: Well, you ought to—I can't stand the color of your hair.

Karen: BILL! You've hurt my feelings!

Bill: *(bashfully)* Oh, I'm sorry. Speaking of laundry, do you know the money changing machines they have in there?

Karen: Well, not personally, but go ahead.

Bill: Well, I wanted to prove how stupid those machines are, so I put a five-dollar bill in one and it still gave me change for a dollar. Just to make sure it was no fluke, I put a ten-dollar bill in the next time and it *still* gave me change for a dollar. I bet you never realized how *stupid* those machines are, did you?

Karen: That doesn't make sense.

Bill: What do you mean?

Karen: I mean you lost thirteen dollars and you are saying the *machines* are stupid.

Bill: Well, I only did it for a change.

Karen: That's what money changers are for—a change.

Bill: That makes sense.

Waiter: I don't mean to interrupt, but are you ready to order?

Bill: Huh?

Waiter: Your order?

Bill: What?

Waiter: ORDER, ORDER!

Bill: What are you, a judge?

Waiter: I don't know about that, but whenever I go to play tennis I wind up in a court.

Bill: You ought to get out of that racket.

Waiter: *(Looks up and states pleadingly:)* Why me? . . . Have you decided what you would like to eat?

Bill:	Yes, I'll take the New York sirloin steak, baked potato, corn, tossed salad with French dressing, and a large Coke. That's all.
Karen:	What about me, Bill?
Bill:	*(surprised)* Aren't you going to buy your own?
Karen:	Of course not; it's not proper.
Bill:	O.K., O.K. Waiter, she'll have a small Coke.
Waiter:	You're not going *overboard*, are you?
Bill:	Don't be silly. We're nowhere near water.
Karen:	You may be right about that—but you're *still* all wet. *(Karen then throws her glass of water all over Bill and they exit.)*

THE COMEDIAN

This is a monologue—that is, a routine for one person. It should be memorized, not read. Timing in the delivery is important.

Here's a second way to use it, which can be a lot of fun: Send four guys out of the room. Bring one of them back in and tell him that you're going to test his abilities as a stand-up comedian. Then read the following script to him, asking him to remember as much of it as he can. Bring the second guy back into the room, and the first guy will perform the routine for him—*without* the written script. The second guy then performs it for the third guy, and so on. By the time the fourth guy gets it, it will be only one paragraph long and so bad it will be hilarious.

You hope.

The Script:

I was born at an early age in a hospital, to be near my mother. We were so poor we didn't live on the other side of the tracks. We lived in the middle. When I was young my folks moved a lot . . . but I always found them.

My mother and father are in the iron-and-steel business. My mother irons and my father steals. Our neighborhood was so bad that when they tore it down, they built slums. I was a tough kid. In fact, I was the only kid on the block who had barbed wire around the top of his playpen. Tough? Hey, man, I was four before I knew I had fingers. And the neighborhood was tough too. Any kid with two ears was new. Any cat with a tail was a tourist. Our favorite game was stick ball in the street. When it rained I played right gutter. I was ugly too. When I was a baby my mother didn't push the baby buggy, she pulled it. I had long curls until I was ten. I wish you could have seen the look on that little boy's face the day I got my hair cut . . . the little boy that used to carry my books to school.

I was in high school when I had my first romance. My first girlfriend was different. She had very affectionate eyes . . . they looked at each other all the time. I won't say she was cross eyed, but every time she cried the tears ran down her back. The doctor called it bacteria. And she had lovely golden hair down her back. None on her head . . . but all down her back. And there was something strange about her teeth. She was the only girl I knew who on Halloween bobbed for applesauce. And she was fat! She sat in my English class . . . in the first two rows. But I didn't mind because anywhere I sat in the room I was next to her. The teacher didn't mind either, because every time my girl turned around she erased the blackboard. We were downtown one day and she got weighed on one of those scales that give your weight on a little card. Hers said "one at a time, please." One day she was wearing a red, white, and blue dress and five people tried to mail a letter. And was she lazy. Every Saturday all she did was sit around the house . . . and she was so bowlegged that she sat around the house. I remember the first time we met. She was sitting on a bench near the cafeteria. I sat down beside her and she cocked an eye at me, I cocked an eye at her and there we sat looking cockeyed at each other. The last I heard of her she had run off with another guy and got married by a Justice of the Peace. After the ceremony the guy asked the Justice of the Peace how much he owed. The Justice said, "Just give me what you think she's worth." So the guy gave him a quarter. The Justice gave him fifteen cents change.

FINE, AND YOU?

This skit is designed for use at Thanksgiving. It is based on the idea that it would have been interesting if the Indians had gone to Europe and discovered the Pilgrims, instead of vice-versa. Explain that premise to the audience to set up the skit: "Have you ever wondered what it would have been like . . ." The scene is somewhere in Europe. Five pilgrims are busy at work when in walks an Indian.

Indian: How?

Pilgrim 1: How what?

Indian: How you doing?

Pilgrim 2: Oh! Fine, and you?

Pilgrim 3: Say, who are you? You don't look like you're from this area.

Indian: I am chief of Sue Bee Indians. I am called Running Water.

Pilgrim 4: Why "Running Water?" Do you have a leaky faucet?

Indian: Yes, my cousin. He been here before?

Pilgrim 5: No, You're the first Indian we've ever seen. Where are you from?

Pilgrim 1: And how did you get here?

Indian: How?

Pilgrim 2: Fine, and you?

Indian: I sail wide river called Atlantic in trusty canoe called April Shower.

Pilgrim 4: There's another funny name. Why did you call your canoe "April Shower"?

Indian: Silly Pilgrim. Don't you know that "April Shower bring Mayflower"?

Pilgrim 3: You still haven't told us where you're from.

Pilgrim 5: Well, he said he sailed across the Atlantic. But of course, we all know that he couldn't come from there since the world is flat and you'd fall if you went in that direction.

Pilgrim 3: Well, maybe he crawled up the edge.

Pilgrim 1: We must be more courteous to our guest. After all, we are preparing to celebrate our harvest.

Indian: Really? How?

Pilgrim 2: Fine, and you?

Pilgrim 1: We set a large table full of food that we have harvested from our crops. Such as corn. *(holding up an ear of corn)*

Indian: Ah, maize.

Pilgrim 4: Did you hear that? He said he was amazed.

Indian: No, no. Maize—that Indian name for what you call "corn."

Pilgrim 4: I just don't understand where you foreigners come up with such funny names for things. I mean, how do you do it?

Indian: How?

Pilgrim 2: Fine, and you?

Pilgrim 5: Say, Leaky Faucet . . .

Pilgrim 4: No, no, that's his cousin's name. He's Running Water.

Pilgrim 5: Well, Leaky Faucet or Running Water. What's the difference? I mean, both names are all wet.

Indian: No. My uncle called All Wet.

Pilgrim 3: You must have a lot of rain back home. I'll have to make you an umbrella to take back with you.

Indian: Make umbrella? You know how?

Pilgrim 2: Fine, and you?

Pilgrim 5: Hey, listen, Running Water. I wanted to ask you, do you Indians plant other things besides corn; like apples, peaches, pumpkins, cherries?

Indian: Oh, yes. But it take long time to plant all these things.

Pilgrim 3: It does? We're able to plant things real fast.

Indian: Oh? How?

Pilgrim 2: Fine, and you?

Pilgrim 3: We use a plow to break up the soil and make the planting faster and easier.

Pilgrim 1: We would be glad to share this knowledge of the plow with you and your family.

Pilgrim 4: Oh, isn't it wonderful to be able to share things with new people from different places.

Indian: And how!

Pilgrim 2: Fine, and you?

Pilgrim 1: Running Water, won't you join us as we celebrate our harvest festival?

Pilgrim 5: Yes, we always have so much that God has given us: good food, good times, good friends.

Pilgrim 3: We have so much to be thankful for.

Indian: Yes. This is time of . . . Thanksgiving.

Pilgrim 4: Thanksgiving! Now, there's one Indian name I really like. I think we should make this a national holiday. *(to Pilgrim 2)* Don't you think so?

Pilgrim 2: Well, yes. But how?

Indian and other Pilgrims: Fine, and you?

THE GREATEST SHOW ON EARTH

Here's a fun skit that contains a grand total of 56 puns guaranteed to bring 56 groans. The cast:

The Announcer
Boss Leland, Owner of the Big Top Circus
Bobo the Clown, Leland's assistant
Bill Blade
Electro, the Human Wall Socket
Nelson Fury, the Human Bullet
Barney Tomb, the Modern Mummy
Creepy Terry Tiptoe, the Tightrope Terror

Announcer: Boss Leland's Big Top Circus has just arrived in the small country town of Grissle. It's time for Boss to organize his troupe of performers. First, he calls for his best friend and trusty sidekick, Bobo the Clown.

Boss: Bobo, do you have any idea what Grissle is like?

Bobo: I hear it's a pretty tough town.

Boss: Really? I find that a bit hard to swallow. But listen, Bobo—the economy is bad, attendance is down, and I just can't afford to keep everybody on my payroll.

	Some of our acts will have to go—I've even made a list. Now, get Bill Blade and bring him here. I want to talk to him about his knife act.
Announcer:	So Bobo brings Bill Blade to Boss. *(They enter.)*
Boss:	Well, well, Bill, don't you look sharp today.
Bill:	It's about my knife act, isn't it, Boss?
Boss:	I'm afraid so. Face it, Bill—your knife act just doesn't cut it around here anymore.
Bobo:	Yeah. It always was a bit dull.
Bill:	Oh, I get the point. You don't think I can hack it. Well, I admit I'm a bit rusty, but I still have an edge on the other performers.
Boss:	I'm sorry, Bill. I've tried to carve you into a competent circus star, but you haven't got the point. No matter how you slice it, it's time for you to switch, Blade.
Announcer:	So Bill Blade sadly leaves his circus home. *(He exits, weeping.)*
Bobo:	I think your words pierced his heart.
Announcer:	Boss now calls in his next candidate: Electro, the Human Wall Socket. *(Enter Electro.)*
Boss:	Electro, I want to talk to you about something.
Electro:	Really, Watt?
Boss:	I have some bad news.
Electro:	If it's about last month's electric bill, I can explain . . .
Boss:	No, that's not it. This may come as a shock to you, but I'm pulling the plug on your act.
Electro:	But why? I've only been here a few weeks. Couldn't you give me an extension?
Boss:	Out of the question.
Electro:	You can't get rid of me that way. I've got connections!
Boss:	Now, don't blow a fuse. You've traveled the whole circuit with us, but due to the current situation, I've got to disconnect you from the Big Top Circus.
Electro:	But I'm the highlight of the show!
Boss:	Go fly a kite, Electro.
Announcer:	So Electro also sadly leaves his circus home. *(He exits.)*
Bobo:	He never was very bright.
Boss:	Who's next on the list?

Bobo:	Nelson Fury, the Human Bullet.
Boss:	He's probably in the powder room. Bring him in. It should be fairly easy to fire the Bullet.
Announcer:	So Bobo, Boss's best buddy, brings Bullet.
Nelson:	Hi, Boss. You want to talk to me?
Boss:	Yes, it's about your act.
Nelson:	My act? Has it triggered something in your mind?
Boss:	Not exactly, Nelson. I realize you're a big shot around here, but I'm letting you go.
Nelson:	But why? My act has always been loaded with excitement. Everyone says it's a barrel of laughs.
Boss:	Be reasonable. Surely a man of your caliber can understand. I've always gotten a bang out of your act, but you'll have to find a new job somewhere else.
Nelson:	I hate to be such a revolver. Shoot!
Announcer:	And so the Human Bullet leaves the Big Top forever. *(He leaves.)*
Boss:	Well, that's the last of him.
Bobo:	The old son-of-a-gun.
Announcer:	Suddenly Bobo is handed some dreadful news!
Bobo:	Boss, I've been handed some dreadful news!
Boss:	What is it?
Bobo:	Barney Tomb, the Modern Mummy, is quitting our circus!
Boss:	What? Bring him here. I want my mummy!
Announcer:	So Bobo brings the Modern Mummy to Boss. *(They enter.)*
Boss:	What's this I hear about you quitting?
Barney:	That's right. I'm getting tired of all this.
Boss:	You're kidding.
Barney:	No, I'm dead serious.
Boss:	You're always so wrapped up in your work. Maybe you need a vacation to unwind a bit. You'd feel a lot better.
Barney:	No, I'm tired of being buried in responsibility. And my health . . . I'm coffin all the time.
Boss:	Where did you dig up *that* excuse?

Barney:	This is a grave situation, Boss. Don't take it lightly. This circus routine bores me stiff.
Boss:	I can't help it if things have been a little dead lately.
Barney:	Don't try shoveling the blame on someone else, Boss. Good-by!
Announcer:	And Barney the Modern Mummy angrily stomps out of the circus. *(Exits.)*
Bobo:	His act never was very lively.
Boss:	Who's next on our list?
Bobo:	Creepy Terry, the Tightrope Terror. I'll go get him.
Announcer:	So Creepy Terry, the Tightrope Terror, tiptoes in to see the Boss. *(He does.)*
Terry:	Hi, Boss. What's up?
Boss:	Terry, I'm afraid your tightrope act is going to take a fall.
Terry:	You're pulling my leg.
Boss:	We're having trouble balancing the budget, and you've been getting out of line lately.
Terry:	That's a lie! I've always been a steady worker. Wire you doing this to me?
Boss:	We're tired of stringing you along.
Terry:	But Boss, I've always walked the line! And don't forget that I've got friends in high places!
Boss:	Sorry, Terry, you're out! We're tired of you acting like you were above us all.
Terry:	I'm a level-headed guy, but you've stretched this too far! I quit!
Announcer:	Creepy Terry tiptoes out of the circus.
Boss:	Well, Bobo, that's the end of our list. In a way it's kinda sad to see them all go.
Bobo:	But Boss, doesn't this play have a happy ending?
Boss:	Sure, Bobo. Everyone will be happy to know that this play is now over.

IN THE HOSPITAL

For this skit, you'll need to set up two tables to be used as hospital beds. Sheets can cover the patients, who should be bandaged up as if they were in terrible shape. A nightstand with some flowers would help set the scene.

The characters:

Bernie, bandaged head and hands
Barbara, the girlfriend
Mrs. Fishbasin, the mother
Emily, the other patient
Nurse, the nurse

Bernie is in bed, very still. Barbara and Mom are on opposite sides of the bed. Emily is in the other bed, covered with a sheet. All we see are her bare feet. She, too, is very still.

Mom: *(leaning over Bernie)* Oh, my poor Bernie. What have they done to you? You should never have left home. This would never have happened if you'd stayed home.

Barbara: (leaning over from her side) He's going to be all right, Mrs. Fishbasin.

Mom: (pulling the bed towards her a little) When you're all well and better you'll come home and we'll give you your old room back.

Barbara: (pulling the bed to her side) Don't be silly, Mrs. Fishbasin. Bernie will be well in plenty of time for us to go ahead with our wedding plans.

Mom: (a more pronounced pull) Marriage, humph. My Bernie is too young to be married. He'll come home when he's got his strength back.

Barbara: (a good solid jerk on the table) My father has already put a down payment on the Moose Hall for the reception!

Mom: (pulling) He's coming home with me!

Barbara: (pulling) No, he isn't!

Nurse: (entering) Ssssshhh!

Mom: (joining in, shooshing Barbara) Sssssshhh!

Nurse: (to both of them) Please! You're going to have to be quieter if you expect to stay. (Exits.)

Mom: (to Barbara) Ssssshhh!

Barbara: (to Bernie, softly) Oh, Bernie . . . Bernie . . . Bernie. Do you remember the day last summer we went to the beach? We had such a good time. We could do that again when you get better.

Mom: (pulling bed to her side again) Bernie, do you remember when you were six years old? I took you to the beach. You said you had the best time you ever had and you didn't want to go to the beach with anybody but me. Ever.

Barbara: (pulling, a louder whisper) He was six!

Mom: (pulling, a still louder whisper) He wouldn't lie to his mother!

Bernie: (Begins to groan.)

Barbara: He's waking up.

Bernie: (groaning slowly) Emily . . . Emily . . . Emily . . .

Barbara: Bernie? It's me, Barbara. The doctors say you're going to be fine. Bernie?

Bernie: (reaching up to feel her face) Emily?

Barbara: Barbara.

Bernie: Emily?

Barbara: Barbara!

Bernie: Emily?

Barbara:	Barbara!
Mom:	Bernie, this is your mother.
Bernie:	(shifting his weight to her side) Emily? (Begins to feel her face.)
Mom:	No, Bernie, your mother.
Bernie:	Emily?
Nurse:	(entering) I'm afraid you're going to have to leave now.
Bernie:	(Leans toward nurse.) Emily?
Nurse:	(to Mom and Barbara) Please—visiting hours are over. You'll have to go.
Mom and Barbara:	(together, but not at the same time) But—
Nurse:	Please.
Mom and Barbara:	(reluctant, but leaving) We'll see you soon, Bernie.
Bernie:	Emily?
Mom and Barbara:	Good night, Bernie. Sleep tight. (Exit.)
Bernie:	Emily . . . Emily . . . Emily . . .
Emily:	(reaching a hand toward Bernie) Bernie?
Bernie:	Emily? (finding hand) Emily.
Emily:	Bernie.
Bernie:	Emily.

KID RINGO

Since this is an "old West" skit, it would be great at a banquet or party where the theme is western. JESSE JONES should be dressed in full cowboy regalia, look mean, and wear his guns low. KID RINGO is a very *old* man who is still trying to live by his legend. He should have spurs and a big hat and should barely be able to get around.

Narrator: In the West of the 1880s, violent men dictated the only law. Those who carried the gun imposed their will upon peaceful men and women. The highest law of the land was written on the barrel of a Colt 44. Often, cruel men preyed upon innocents, taking whatever they wanted. But sometimes, men of the gun met each other in battle for prize, possession, or reputation. These "showdowns" were terrible clashes—the poetry of destruction as written by the pen of hate dipped in an inkwell of blood.

Jesse:	(He stops at stage, takes out his gun, checks it carefully by rotating the cylinder, then holsters it again. He frees his shoulder and arm muscles by several stretches and shrugs. He then loosens up his hands and cracks his knuckles. Now satisfied that he is ready, he sets himself with a mean look and a slight crouch, hands ready at his guns. He yells.) Kid! Kid Ringo! I'm callin' you out! (no answer) (louder) Kid, I know you're in there! It's me, Jesse Jones. You've eluded me long enough. You're goin' to meet me in the street today and the devil in hades tonight, Kid! (The door opens and Kid Ringo begins to come out onto the stage. He shuffles slowly up.)
Kid:	The "devil in hades," huh? You cain't say that in front of all these ladies.
Jesse:	(incredulously) I cain't? I just did!
Kid:	Well, I guess you got a point there. (He turns and begins to leave.)
Jesse:	Where you goin'?
Kid:	Back to watch the girls go by in the hotel lobby.
Jesse:	Why?

Kid:	I don't remember.
Jesse:	Get back here and prepare to throw hot lead. *(He takes a step or two toward Kid and spurs jingle.)*
Kid:	What's the funny noise?
Jesse:	Them's ma' spurs. Don't you wear spurs, Kid?
Kid:	Don't wear 'em anymore after the wife died.
Jesse:	Never mind, Ringo—I've killed 37 men and I'm aimin' to make you 38. How many've you killed?
Kid:	Let's see . . . *(Begins to count slowly on hands, then drops down to take off one boot. When he starts taking off second boot, Jesse interrupts.)*
Jesse:	*(mad)* Never mind, you old coot, reach for your guns.
Kid:	Wait a minute, I'm not warm yet. *(Kid goes through a warm-up procedure like Jesse, except for the gun. When he tries to crack his knuckles, he is unable to do so for lack of strength. Finally he puts his hands under his boots and tries to stand up.)*
Jesse:	C'mon, Kid—go for your gun!
Kid:	Not so fast. Let's do it the old way. Back to back, we take five paces, turn, draw, and fire.
Jesse:	I don't care how I kill you, let's just do it. *(They come together at stage center, turn back to back.)*
Jesse:	Ready? One, two, three, four, five! *(He turns and begins to draw . . . but Kid Ringo is still shuffling and beginning to turn around.)* You're not even ready, you dumb old coot! Just back away. I'll give you a chance. You can draw first. When I count three, you go for your gun. O.K.?
Kid:	O.K.
Jesse:	One! Two! Three! *(pause)* Well, go for your gun.
Kid:	I am. *(His hand slowly creeps toward his gun.)*
Jesse:	This is the last chance I'm givin' you, Kid. No more stallin'. You better be ready, 'cause this time I'm pullin' down on you. Are you loaded?
Kid:	I wish I were.
Jesse:	Nah, I mean the gun, stupid.
Kid:	Wait a minute, I'll see. *(He pulls his gun out and twirls the cylinder. The barrel is pointed away toward front of stage. As he checks the gun, it goes off. One of*

the spectators on the front row gasps and slides off the chair, clutching his chest.)

Jesse: Now you've done it. You've killed an innocent bystander. You're the worst gunfighter I've ever seen. Don't you even know how to use a gun?

Kid: I didn't mean to . . . I was just checkin' my gun and it went off. It must have a bad trigger or something. *(He's pointing the gun down and towards Jesse, and it fires. Jesse groans and slumps to the floor toward the Kid so that he's almost at his feet. The Kid is unaware that Jesse has been shot.)* Did it again. I better fight you before I shoot all my bullets. *(Turns toward where Jesse stood and squints, trying to see him.)* Where'd he go? Run off like all them others. *(Holsters gun.)* Yup, they all turns to jelly in their boots when they face up to KID RINGO. *(Shuffles offstage.)*

LITTLE RED RIDING HOOD

This skit requires only two characters. One is a guy dressed up like "Little Red Riding Hood." (Have him wear a red raincoat with a hood or red scarf.) The other is the wolf (dressed in black). Little Red has a basket covered with a towel. Inside the basket is a blank (starter's) gun. Little Red skips into the room with her basket. . . .

Red: *(to audience)* I'm Little Red Riding Hood and I'm going to gramma's house with this basket of goodies! *(Skips around the stage area.)*

Wolf: *(entering, and jumping in front of Red)* Boo!

Red: EEK! EEK! Boy, are you ugly!

Wolf: I'm the big bad wolf and I'm going to eat you all up!

Red: But I'm just poor Little Red Riding Hood and I'm going to gramma's house with this basket of goodies. You wouldn't want to disappoint poor old gramma now, would you?

Wolf: You got a point there. I'll let you go this time. Maybe I'll run into the three pigs somewhere along the way.

Red Riding Hood skips off around the room and the wolf turns to the audience.

Wolf: Ha ha ha—what Little Red Riding Hood doesn't know is that I'm gonna beat her to gramma's house. I'll take a shortcut through the strawberry patch . . . sort of a "strawberry shortcut. . . ."

The wolf gets under a blanket on the floor and Red Riding Hood arrives.

Red: Knock! Knock!
Wolf: *(in a high voice)* Who's there?
Red: Yah!
Wolf: Yah who? Aw, just come on in already.
Red: Hi, gramma. Gee, what big ears you have, gramma.
Wolf: What? Oh, yeah . . . all the better to hear you with, my dear.
Red: And what big eyes you have, gramma.
Wolf: All the better to see you with, my dear, heh-heh!

Red: And what a big nose you have, gramma.

Wolf: All the better to smell your goodies with, my dearie.

Red: And what big teeth you have, gramma.

Wolf: *(Jumps out from the blanket.)* Yeah! All the better to eat you with . . . !

Red Riding Hood pulls the gun out of the basket and shoots about six shots into the wolf.

Wolf: *(Staggers, falls to his knees.)* Well, folks, the moral of this story is . . . "Little girls just ain't as dumb as they used to be." *(Falls.)*

THE LONE STRANGER

This skit, of course, is a takeoff on the old Lone Ranger show. The only props you'll really need are some homemade costumes for the Ranger (a powder blue suit, white hat, black gloves, mask and gun) and Toronto (a basic Indian outfit), two play stick-horses, a recording of the William Tell Overture, and some black makeup to paint another mask underneath the Ranger's real mask. A gun with some blanks or caps and some arrows made from coat hangers so they fit around a person's waist would help. Be sure that the actors are quick-witted and have memorized their parts well and that the narrator reads his or her part with gusto.

Narrator: *(onstage as William Tell Overture plays)* In times past, life was rugged in the old wild west. The law of the land was the law of the gun. But in those days there were two who stood for law and order. (with great intensity) With a cloud of light and the speed of dust and a hearty "Ohio Sliver, Away!" it was the Lone Stranger and his faithful Indian companion, Toronto.

Return with us now to those thrilling days of yesteryear as the Lone Stranger rides again. But first, a word from our sponsor. *(Holds up can of deodorant.)*

Here's a product to delight everyone—guaranteed to keep your present friends close by your side and, with continued use, to make you new friends. Don't go anywhere without it. You'll like the new improved formula and the tangy scent—"early autumn burnt leaves." This product has the seal of approval from the Environmental Protection Agency. Give your armpits a thrill today and save yourself some "scents" with Smell Guard deodorant spray. (Pause.)

Our story opens as Lone and Toronto are riding their horses, Sliver and Scoot, from their latest escapade toward the town of Stiff City, a real dead town. They are talking . . .

Lone: Ah, Toronto, here we are riding again.

Toronto: Yes, Kimoslobby, it seem we always start episode this way.

Lone: It's been a rough ride—through the mud, through the desert, over mountains . . .

Toronto: Mmmm. Me never understand how your horse always stay white. My horse white once, too, but that many moons ago.

Lone: Toronto, why do you always talk about moons—are you a lunatic?

Toronto: No, just in a daze.

Lone: Well, what's on the schedule for today?

Toronto: (Pulls out black book.) Let me look, Kimoslobby.

Lone: (to audience) I wish I knew what that word meant. He's been calling me that ever since we left Tombstone.

Toronto: Mmmm. Shirley and Doris . . . Oh, wrong page! (Turns page.) Ah, this more like it. Look like we fight Bingo Boys this week. They escape from prison yesterday.

Lone: The Bingo Boys, eh? Two real cards. Given a life sentence for running an illegal bingo operation on the boardwalk of Dodge City. Their days are numbered.

Toronto: Me remember their prison numbers—B-8, G-9.

Lone: (Pulls out bingo card.) B-8, G-9. BINGO!

Toronto: Don't start, Kimoslobby. (Gunshots ring out.)

Lone: Did you hear that, Toronto? Was that gunshots?

Toronto: No, dummy—my horse backfire. (to audience) Of all rangers, me have to get stuck with Masked Marvel. Him come from crazy tepee, if you know what I mean. (Makes "he's a nut" sign to audience, pointing at head.)

Lone: The stage is being robbed! It's the Bingo Boys! Ohio, Sliver! (Exits.)

Toronto: (puzzled) Ohio? (then) Massachusetts, Scoot! (Exits.)

Narrator: Lone and Toronto hurry to the stage. It was the Bingo Boys, all right. They had robbed the stage. As usual, Lone and Toronto arrive too late to help.

Toronto:	Why we always arrive too late?
Lone:	Your horse always slows us down.
Toronto:	Scoot good horse. Training wheels slow Scoot down. *(As Lone drives up to stage driver, the driver sticks hands up in the air.)*
Driver:	You're too late, masked man.
Lone:	Don't worry. This mask's on the side of the law and always will be.
Toronto:	Be glad he wear mask. Believe me, he look better with mask.
Lone:	What did they take, Driver?
Driver:	*(Goes into crying act.)* Everything. Horses, guns, stage, props, scenery.
Toronto:	By George, he strip stage!
Driver:	*(quickly back to composure)* They're setting up a traveling bbngo show in Stiff City as soon as they get some money and prizes.
Lone:	Let's head to Stiff City quickly, Toronto. Ohio, Sliver! *(Exits.)*
Toronto:	Kentucky, Scoot! *(Exits.)*

Narrator: Now a word from our sponsor, Scrape Shaving Cream. Scrape removes the chief cause of your whiskers—your face! No brush, no lather, no rub-in . . . just blood.

Now back to our episode, so to speak. Toronto and Lone are at the Sheriff's office in Stiff City.

(As Lone enters, Sheriff puts hands in air.)

Sheriff:	Take whatever you want, mister, just leave my pretty badge.
Lone:	Don't worry. This mask's on the side of the law and always will be.
Toronto:	*(to audience)* Haven't we heard that somewhere before?
Lone:	*(handing sheriff a bullet)* Does this mean anything to you?
Sheriff:	No, does this mean anything to you? *(He dances.)*
Toronto:	Oh, that easy—latest rain dance.
Sheriff:	Shucks, he guessed. *(Looks closely at bullet.)* Well, well, a chrome bullet. What's this say? *(Reads bullet.)* "Made in Japan." There's only one man who carries a chrome bullet made in Japan. *(pause)* So where'd *you* get it, clod?
Lone:	Yes, a chrome bullet. Silver's expensive these days.

Sheriff:	*(Hits him all of a sudden.)* Why, it's the Lone Stranger. I never would have known you without the Indian.
Lone:	Yes, it's me. We're after the Bingo Boys. They're heading this way.
Deputy:	*(Runs in.)* Sheriff, somebody just held up the bank!
Lone:	Someone's holding up the bank?
Toronto:	That mighty heavy bank.
Sheriff:	Last guy that did that got a hernia.
Lone:	What happened? Can you give me an account?
Toronto:	Oh, leave him a loan.
Lone:	I was only checking. I wanted to see his interest.
Toronto:	It not his vault. You just compounding the problem!

Narrator:	We leave this exciting moment for a word from the makers of Scrunchies. You've heard of the breakfast of champions? Well, Scrunchies are for people who just want to get into the semifinals. Scrunchies contain 20% iron, 30% copper, 15% steel, and 55% zinc. They don't snap, crackle, and pop—they just lie there and rust.
	Now let us return to Lone and Toronto. They enter the bank.

(As Lone enters, tellers put up hands.)

Teller:	There's nothing left to take, mister.
Lone:	Don't worry. This mask's on the side of the law and always will be. *(As Lone speaks, Toronto mimics every line silently and gives audience a look of disgust.)* I'd like $50.00 in Traveler's Checks.
Teller:	American Express?
Toronto:	Never leave home without them. *(Teller gives Lone checks, and Lone exits. Toronto starts to exit, then turns back to teller.)* How much you give for pure white horse?

Narrator:	Lone and Toronto leave the town and head for their camp in the hills. We meet them there. . . .

Toronto:	Lone, can I ask question?
Lone:	Sure, go ahead.
Toronto:	Why you call me Toronto when my real name is Fred?
Lone:	Well . . .
Toronto:	And why we always camp outside in dusty hills when Holiday Inn right down the road?
Lone:	Shhh, I hear something.

(Two Indians ride into camp; they see Lone and raise their hands.)

Lone:	Don't worry. This mask's on the side of the law and always will be.
Toronto:	*(directing audience)* Altogether now. *(They repeat Stranger's favorite line.)*
Chief:	*(in a sissy voice)* Me Chief Fire Mouth.
Toronto:	We can tell. *(Coughs from breath.)*
Chief:	*(Points to other Indian.)* This my friend, Running Nose. *(He sneezes.)*
Chief:	We in heap big trouble.
Lone:	You mean a whole lot.
Chief:	No, not a whole lot, just a little lot. About ten-acre reservation on other side of hill.
Lone:	What happened?
Chief:	Bingo Boys. Steal all our ceramic kits. We won them in a raffle.
Toronto:	Oh, pottery lottery.
Chief:	That right. How we make souvenirs for white men now? Can you help us?
Lone:	I think so. You go back to reservation and tell your braves to keep calm. We'll think of something. *(Chief and Indian exit.)*
Lone:	You have two options, Toronto. One, you could go keep the Indians calm.
Toronto:	Can't do that. Couldn't get close to them. Need reservation.
Lone:	Then you'll have to go into town and see if you can get more help.
Toronto:	Why always me go into town? I always get shot or put in jail. You go this time.
Lone:	No, I have to stay here.
Toronto:	Let me put it this way. How would you feel as only Indian in white man town?
Lone:	Yes, but . . .
Toronto:	I tell Chief Fire Mouth you call him "sissy."

Lone: *(That hits Lone hard.)* That's different. Well, I guess we'll have to hit the trail together. *(which they do, banging on ground)*

Narrator: As we leave our banging heroes we want to remind you that the National Traffic Council says that about 555 people will die on our highways this week. So far only 320 have died. Some of you aren't trying.
             Now we return to Lone and Toronto. They're tracking the gang.

(Toronto with head on ground, listening)

Lone: You hear anything? *(pause)* I don't see anything.

(Two outlaws come running in, right over top of Toronto.)

Toronto: Me think me hear something.

Narrator: Now a word from an alternate sponsor, Neversharp, the greatest name in ball point pens. Get the seventy-five dollar model that writes over butter, or the dollar-ninety-eight model that writes over margarine. Neversharp has the only meatball point for writing in spaghetti. Neversharp—the dull pen for the man with a pointed head.
             Well, back to our story. Because of their effective tracking technique, Lone and Toronto soon catch up to the outlaws, the Bingo Boys, and corner them in the Grand Canyon. Disaster strikes, however, as Lone, sure of foot but not of mind, is separated from Toronto and is captured by the Bingo Boys. Is this the end of our hero? Has he reached the last round up? Is he headed toward that big stranger station in the sky?

Outlaw #1:   All, right. This is it, stranger.
Outlaw #2:   Yeah. Your jig is up.
Lone: It is? Is it showing? *(Tugs at pantlegs.)*
Outlaw #1:   All right. Off with the mask.
Lone: *(to audience)* I love this next line. *(to outlaw)* I wouldn't do that if I were you.

Outlaw #1:	Aw, shut up. *(The Big Moment! He removes mask—only to reveal another mask painted on Lone's face.)*
Outlaw #2:	Let's shoot him anyway.
Lone:	*(looking up at canyon walls)* Wow. Indians all over the place.
Outlaw #1:	Oh, no, we're goners.
Toronto:	*(riding up)* That right. Dropum youum gunums.
Lone:	Nice work, Toronto. Remind me to give you an English lesson later. I didn't think you'd get the whole Apache tribe to help us out.
Toronto:	What help? I told Chief you call him "sissy." *(They exit—quickly.)*
Narrator:	In short order, the Lone Stranger and Toronto bring the Bingo Boys to justice as well as hold off ten thousand wild Apaches. They return to Stiff City to bid farewell to the Sheriff.
Lone:	Well, it's adios, Sheriff.
Toronto:	Why you speak Spanish all of sudden? Me have enough trouble with English.
Sheriff:	You've done us a great favor.
Toronto:	*(accompanying speech with sign language gestures)* Yes, as my father once said, "When bull run with geese through tall grass, then wild trees will jump on tepee while empty buckets fly over mountainside."
Sheriff:	*(puzzled)* What?
Lone:	Crime doesn't pay. Adios.

(As they leave, in turning they reveal arrows all over back, remnants of fight with Apaches.)

Deputy:	Who was that masked man?
Sheriff:	*(long pause while looking at Lone and Toronto exiting—then:)* Beats me!

(William Tell Overture comes on.)

Narrator:	Once again the Lone Stranger and his faithful Indian companion, Toronto, have made the world a little safer for democracy. The daring masked man of the plains rides on in his quest for truth, justice, and the American way! *(pause)* Wait a minute, I got the wrong show. Well, anyway, adios!

THE MAD REPORTER

The scene is the Golden Gate Bridge. A very depressed newspaper reporter is about to jump. (The edge of a stage or platform can be used as the edge of the bridge.)

Characters:

Reporter
Woman
Teenager
Man

Reporter:	I've had it. I'm all washed up. Two years on the newspaper staff and not a single big story. I'm going to jump off this bridge and end it all! *(Starts to jump, but stops when woman enters . . .)*
Woman:	Life is terrible. My husband doesn't love me. My kids can't stand me. I'm a failure in everything I do. Even the women's liberation movement is against me. *(Cries.)*
Reporter:	Why don't you just jump off this bridge with me? I'm going to end it all.
Woman:	You're right. Let's go. *(counting together)* One . . . Two . . . *(Teenager enters.)*
Teenager:	Life is really a drag. I just can't go on this way. What do I have to look forward to? Nothing. Overpopulation. Pollution. Wars. Poverty. We can send men to the moon, but I can't find a job. I've had it . . .
Reporter:	Excuse me, but I couldn't help overhearing. We're going to end it all by jumping off the bridge here. Why don't you join us?
Teenager:	Gladly.
All:	One . . . Two . . . Three . . . *(Stop when man enters.)*
Man:	What am I going to do? The stock market left me broke. My wife has run away with the milkman. I lost my job. My house burned down. Nothing but reruns on television . . .
Reporter:	Hey, mister. We're going to end it all right now. It's the easiest way out.
Man:	Good idea.
All:	One . . . Two . . . Three . . . JUMP! *(They all jump except the reporter).*

Reporter: Wow! What a story! Three people jump to their deaths! I can see it now on the front page! Wait till the boss sees this! *(Exits.)*

ONE FINE DAY IN A DISASTROUS FLOOD

Only two characters are needed for this one—Noah and his son Ham. Unless you can get a 450-foot ark made out of gopher wood, the only other prop you'll need is a can of Coke. The play begins with Noah and Ham walking onto the stage; both rocking back and forth as though they are on a boat. Ham looks sick.

Ham: *(groan)* Ohhhhh. . .
Noah: What seems to be the trouble, Ham, my boy?
Ham: I don't feel so good.
Noah: You don't look so good either. Why?
Ham: It smells in here. These animals smell worse than a dead skunk in a heat wave.
Noah: Oh, come now. It can't be all that bad, just because we have two of every animal in the world in this ark.
Ham: Well, that's not all. This boat is going back and forth and back and forth. We've been in here three hundred and twenty-six days, twelve hours, three minutes, and seventeen seconds. We've been floating in this water so long I'm starting to feel like a teabag.
Noah: Hey, don't worry, son. I don't think God's going to keep us in here too much longer. Have patience.
Ham: Well, maybe for another forty-nine days, eleven hours, and possibly fifty-seven minutes and forty-three seconds.
Noah: Is it still raining outside?
Ham: Does it ever rain on the inside?
Noah: No respect, no respect.
Ham: Take a peek and see.
Noah: *(Looks out window.)* It's raining so hard I can't see what the weather's like.
Ham: Let me see, Dad. *(Looks out window.)* Why, it's raining cats and dogs outside.
Noah: Son, I told you to keep those animals inside the ark.

Ham: That was only a figure of speech. It sure rains a lot.

Noah: Yes, son, I think we're over the future site of Seattle, Washington. That reminds me, I think I left the water running in the bathtub back home.

Ham: Uh oh, Dad. When we get the water bill, Mom's going to kill you!

Noah: I hope you meant that as a figure of speech.

Ham: Hey, Dad—do boats sink often?

Noah: Only once.

Ham: What if we get a hole in the ark and it sinks?

Noah: Impossible. For one thing, God wouldn't allow us to sink; that would ruin the whole story. Besides, I can't swim.

Ham: What if we do sink? We don't have any life preservers big enough to fit the elephants.

Noah: Oh, you're such a ham, Ham. Trust God. He's holding this boat together.

Ham: But things are just so dull around here. I wake up in the morning to the rooster's crow, the pig's oink, and to the zebra's . . . whatever noise they make. Have you ever tried to get a six-hundred-pound Siberian tiger to use a kitty litter box? Don't. Also Dad, you've got to do something about those dive-bombing birds. I have to wash my hair every hour because of them. Speaking of which, have you seen my hair dryer lying around the ark anyplace?

Noah: Yes, I have. While I was drying my beard with it, the ostrich swallowed it . . . shocking sight.

Ham: You're kidding. I don't know how much more of this I can handle.

Noah: What, this ark?

Ham: No, your jokes.

Noah: Like I said before, you must have patience.

Ham: Oh, I have patience. I've always had patience. Ever since I was born I've had patience. *(pause)* What's patience?

Noah: Patience is the suffering of affliction with a calm, unruffled temper. When you're patient through times of trial and tribulation, God will shape and mold you into a new and better you.

Ham: But, Dad, I'm so bored. This whole place is totally boring. I want off this ark.

Noah: But, son, don't you want to grow?

Ham: What do you mean? Does being bored help me to grow? That's totally wild; I suppose if I was excited it would stunt my growth.

Noah: No, son, I don't mean that kind of growth. I'm talking about spiritual growth. You see, through each trial and tribulation we should praise God because we can benefit spiritually and grow to be a stronger Christian for God. So just be patient until the great rainbow in the sky shines bright.

Ham: Thanks, Dad. I'll go finish cleaning out the stalls.

Noah: Hurry up; Mom's cooking dinner.

Ham: What are we having?

Noah: What do you want?

Ham: Barbecued barley with cheese sauce.

Noah: Want a side order of fries with that?

Ham: No, thanks—maybe some alfalfa sprouts topped with ketchup.

Noah: You've got it.

Ham: Oh, by the way, Dad, have you seen any dry land yet?

Noah: I sent a raven out earlier this morning to find dry land, but that raven had aquatic phobia. *(to the audience)* That's the fear of water. With the water below him and the rain around him, that bird totally freaked out.

Ham: Why don't we try it again, only with a smaller animal?

Noah: I know. I'll use a snake.

Ham:	Naaa, Harold's got a cold. Besides, that snake is so nearsighted he fell deeply in love with a rope.
Noah:	I bet his love life is all tied up.
Ham:	Why don't we use a dove?
Noah:	Naaa, that won't work. *(pause)* I know, we'll use a dove.
Ham:	*(to himself)* Why didn't I think of that?
Noah:	Here, pretty bird. *(Noah acts as if he's reaching into a cage for a dove.)* Now listen carefully. I want you to fly out and find dry ground, and if you do find dry ground, bring something back as proof. Good luck and God be with you. *(Throws the dove out the window.)* Fly and be free. *(Mime watching the bird fly, then fall down into the water.)* Swim, swim, flap your wings like this. *(Flap arms.)* That's it, go, go, go. *(to son)* Remind me to sign that bird up for the next Olympics.
Ham:	Right.
Noah:	Look.
Ham:	Where?
Noah:	Up there! The dove is returning, and it has something in its beak. *(A can of Coke is thrown on stage; Noah catches it.)* Look, the dove has found land.
Ham:	*(Grabs the Coke can and holds it out to the audience.)* It's the real thing!
Noah:	*(Noah sings part of the Coke jingle.)* Coca-Cola . . . oh, anyway, I knew God wouldn't let us down; you just got to have . . .
Ham:	I know, I know, have patience.
Noah:	You've got it now, my boy. Oh, no!
Ham:	What?
Noah:	Oh, no!
Ham:	WHAT!
Noah:	I hope we can find a hotel with a vacant room.
Ham:	Don't worry, I bet a lot of people stayed home because of the rain. *(They exit.)*

THE PSYCHIATRIST

This is a skit that requires two people: the psychiatrist and his patient. The scene is the doctor's office. The only props needed are a couch (for the patient to lie down on) and a chair for the doctor. The skit begins with a knock on the doctor's door, and he answers it.

Man: Oh, hello there. Are you Dr. Kaseltzer, the psychiatrist?

Doc: Yes I am, and that will be twenty dollars. What other questions can I help you with?

Man: Well, my name is Mr. Gaspocket. . . . I have an appointment.

Doc: Oh, yes. What's the nature of your problem?

Man: Well, I'm trying to break—bark!—a nervous habit.

Doc: Well, maybe I can help you.

Man: Thanks, doc—bark!

Doc: How long has this been going on?

Man: Ever since I was a teenager—bark!

Doc: Hmmm. Think back. Were you ever frightened by a vicious dog?

Man: Why?

Doc: Well, these problems can often be traced to some single event.

Man: No, this is just a—bark!—nervous habit.

Doc: Have you ever tried to break it before?

Man: Oh, yes, I've tried lots of things, such as wearing gloves.

Doc: Wait a minute. You've tried wearing gloves?

Man: Yes. Well, you know, I thought if I would start wearing gloves, I might stop biting my nails.

Doc: Biting your nails?

Man: Well, yes. That's the nervous habit I was telling you about.

Doc: You mean you came to see me just because you bite your nails?

Man: Well, certainly. What else—bark!—what else in the world—bark!—would I have on my mind?

Doc: Maybe you should lie down here and tell me all about it.

Man: Well, I'm not allowed on the furniture.

Doc: That's all right, I don't mind.

Man: Well, all right. You see, one reason I get nervous and bite my nails is—bark!—because of my mother.

Doc: Your mother?

Man: Well, she always made me sleep on a bunch of newspapers down in the cellar. Somehow, she got this crazy quirk, you know, she got it in her mind—now you won't believe this—but she imagined that I went around the house—now listen to this—that I went around the house *barking* like a dog!

Doc:	You think she imagined this?
Man:	Well, I *know* she did. She finally wrote to a doctor about me ... a veterinarian.
Doc:	Oh, really? And what did he say?
Man:	I don't know. I never let the mailman near the house—bark! bark!
Doc:	This goes deeper than I thought. I'm going to try the word association test. I'll say a word and you say the first word that comes to your mind. ... Table.
Man:	Chair.
Doc:	Ball.
Man:	Bat.
Doc:	Flower.
Man:	Rose.
Doc:	Cat.
Man:	Bark!
Doc:	Dogcatcher.
Man:	Bark! Bark! Bark!
Doc:	Hmmm. This is going to require some consultation. Why don't you come in next Thursday?
Man:	Oh, no, Doc—couldn't you make it another day? I don't want to miss "Lassie."
Doc:	Okay. How about Sunday night around 6?
Man:	Nope, that's *(announce youth group)*.
Doc:	O.K. Let's make it Monday. Good day, sir.
Man:	*(Exits.)* Bark! Bark!

TARZAN

This skit takes place "in the jungle," of course. As it opens, Tarzan's boy companion, Jive, is tied to a pole, ready to be burned at the stake.

Characters:

Tarzan *(dressed in loincloth)*
Colonel Grub, the villain *(in safari outfit)*

Chief (*dressed in African native garb*)
Jive, Tarzan's boy companion
Tenderbelly, the chief's daughter
Narrator

Narrator: Darkest Africa! Wild and foreboding! Man-killing beasts stalk their prey in these dark jungles, ready at any moment to spring, tear, and mangle. Wild savages lurk in dense underbrush waiting to ambush unwary travelers. So sit right back and relax, as we present "Tarzan."

Colonel: (*to audience*) Hi, there! I'm the villain in tonight's episode! So far, I've burned down the village of the Lumbago Tribe, I've captured Tarzan's little friend Jive, and, worst of all, I've said nasty things to the animals! But, so far, Tarzan hasn't shown up!

Tarzan: (*Tarzan enters, swinging on a rope if possible, and yelling.*) AHHH . . . EEEEE . . . AHHH . . . EEEEE . . . AHHH . . . WAAYA!

Colonel:	Oh-Oh! That's Tarzan now! *(to Tarzan)* Me Colonel Grub! You Tarzan! Tarzan want boy to live? Tarzan listen to me! Me Boss! You Slave! Savvy?
Tarzan:	Tell me, Colonel, have you had this speech problem all your life?
Colonel:	Why—Why, you speak as good as me!
Tarzan:	Wrong again, Colonel! That's "as well as I." And I happen to speak *better* than you.
Colonel:	But when did all this happen? What happened to your English?
Tarzan:	Well, Jane isn't with me any longer, so I spend my evenings brushing up on my English!
Colonel:	Well, good English or bad English, the situation remains the same! Either you take orders from me or the boy dies!
Tarzan:	Big deal! I hardly know the kid! *(Chief enters.)*
Chief:	Ungowah! Tarzan in big trouble! Tarzan burn down village of Lumbagos!
Tarzan:	I didn't burn down your village!
Chief:	We put Tarzan in cobra pit. If Tarzan speak truth, cobra will not kill!
Tarzan:	Cobra pit? Isn't it enough if I say, "Cross my heart and hope to die?"
Colonel:	What are you afraid of, Tarzan? I've heard that you're the friend of a million jungle animals!
Tarzan:	I am! Unfortunately there are a million and a half in this jungle! Besides, it was probably *you* who burned this village.
Colonel:	Maybe! But how are you going to prove it?
Tarzan:	With my knowledge of the jungle, it would be easy to follow footprints, search for matches and gasoline in your tent, investigate ashes . . .
Colonel:	Resorting to evidence, eh? The oldest trick in the book! But it won't work among these savages! They believe in the judgment of the cobra! So into the pit!
Tarzan:	What are you going to do with the boy?
Chief:	He stay tied up! Any friend of Tarzan's no friend of ours!
Tarzan:	That's unfair! Why not put the kid in with the cobra and tie me up to the tree?
Jive:	Tarzan! How can you talk like that! I've been at your side every waking moment for the past nine years!
Tarzan:	Which is precisely why I'm talking like this!
Chief:	Enough! Into the pit! *(Tarzan exits.)*

Narrator:	Once in the pit, our fearless hero gains the friendship of the cobra, once more proving that all jungle animals love Tarzan. *(Tarzan enters with snake over shoulder.)*
Chief:	Ancient tribal code say, since Tarzan make friend with cobra, Tarzan must be telling truth!
Colonel:	Hold on, Chief! I wanted Tarzan to help me trap elephants for ivory! But I don't need him! Your tribe can help me instead! Follow my orders and I'll make you rich!
Chief:	However, modern tribal code say, since you offer us good deal, ancient tribal code don't stand a chance! We follow!
Tarzan:	Don't do it, Chief! Don't you see this man's intentions are dubious, insidious, and furtive?!
Colonel:	And my first order as your leader is to kill the loinclothed Noah Webster!
Tarzan:	Stop! After years of companionship and understanding, you can't kill me like that! You aren't that savage!
Chief:	Right! We must repay him for his kindness! Count to five . . . then kill!
Narrator:	Tarzan, realizing that he is doomed, proceeds to bellow out one of his famous earsplitting jungle cries . . . this momentarily deafens those around him, enabling him to flee to freedom among the familiar jungle surroundings. *(Tarzan flees.)*
Colonel:	Well, Jive! It looks like your friend Tarzan isn't coming back to help you! Any last requests?
Jive:	Yes! Would you please remove my draft card from my pocket before you light the fire? I don't want to get into trouble for burning my draft card.
Tarzan:	Now to see what Colonel Grub is up to! Holy ant hills! They're going to burn Jive at the stake! If I didn't have laundry to do I'd rescue him! Wait a minute! Jive does my laundry! Darn! Now I've got to save him!
Tarzan:	O.K., Colonel! Drop the gun!
Chief:	O.K., Tarzan! Drop the knife!
Colonel:	You'll be sorry you came back, Tarzan! O.K., Chief! Run him through!
Tarzan:	Wait, Chief! I appeal to you!
Chief:	Sorry! Tarzan do not appeal to me! Not even in that miniskirt!

Tenderbelly:	Wait! Stop! Spare Tarzan's life! Kill me instead!
Tarzan:	Tenderbelly! You're the Chief's daughter! Why do you want to save my life!
Tenderbelly:	Because Tarzan teach me how to love, kiss, and make out!
Tarzan:	Tenderbelly! Please! Don't say another word!
Tenderbelly:	Tenderbelly's big heart say Tarzan must live!
Tarzan:	Yeah . . . but Tenderbelly's big mouth say Tarzan must die.
Chief:	Enough fooling around! We settle this mess with big fight to finish! If Tarzan loses and is killed, then he must be put to death!
Tarzan:	Your sentence structure is a trifle redundant, Chief! Grammatically speaking the proper phrasing should be . . .
Chief:	Hold your filthy tongue in front of the maiden! Have you no respect for an innocent girl? The iron tooth will show the truth!
Tarzan:	You mean that knife will decide my life?!
Colonel:	Enough dumb rhyme! You're wasting time! *(Tenderbelly shoots the Colonel.)*
Tenderbelly:	The job is done! I used the gun!
Chief:	One more poem and I go home!
Tarzan:	Tenderbelly! How could you kill him like that?
Tenderbelly:	I knew you couldn't! You too chicken! Besides, after you spare him, he turn around and stab you in back!
Chief:	Tenderbelly speak the truth! I was blinded by promises of wealth! But now, Colonel Grub is dead, and Tarzan lives! Tarzan do another show next week! And week after that! And summer reruns! Chief no fool! He know which side of bread to butter up! *(Chief exits.)*
Jive:	Tarzan, I'm free! They set me free!
Tarzan:	Well, I can console myself with the knowledge that there will always be other villains willing to kill a kid!
Jive:	What can I do to repay you for saving my life?
Tarzan:	Just a simple token of appreciation will be enough! Like a whalebone slingshot!
Jive:	But the nearest whales are millions of miles from here . . . in the Arctic!
Tarzan:	Dress warmly, kid! As for you, Tenderbelly . . . I think we should continue your lessons! *(Tarzan and Tenderbelly exit.)*

Narrator: So as Tarzan and Tenderbelly frolic through the underbrush together, we come to the end of tonight's episode of ... TARZAN!

THE THREE PIGS

Here's a skit about the three little pigs that requires only two pigs and a wolf.

Characters:

Announcer
Practical Pig
Bolivar Pig
Wolf

Announcer: Once upon a time, in a faroff land, there lived three little pigs who were in the construction business. The older brother, Practical, was President and General Manager. The middle brother was named Bolivar and managed the twigs division, and the younger brother, a wee little fellow named Irving, was manager of the straw division. They worked hard and developed a tidy little business. They built some outstanding buildings, solid substantial dwellings—monuments to men's ingenuity and building skill—such as the County Courthouse, National Bowling Lanes, and the outhouses on the *(name of your town)* Mall. On the day of our story, a new construction contract was causing no end of confusion in the three pigs' office.

Practical: Bolivar, we can't build those doghouses out of straw, and that's final. The dogs might smoke in bed. Honestly, you are the dumbest person I ever met. In fact, you are very close to an idiot.
Bolivar: So—don't stand so close to me. I'm not so stupid.
Practical: Oh, yeah? I bet that even during football season you can't tell me the most common use for pigskin.
Bolivar: I can too.

Practical:	What?
Bolivar:	To hold pigs together.
Practical:	Just a minute, Bolivar—how come you were late for work last night?
Bolivar:	Well, it was so foggy I ran into a cow.
Practical:	Was it a Jersey cow?
Bolivar:	I don't know—I didn't see her license plate. She was an udder mess. Say, Practical, there's a guy out here to see you. Says he wants a job.
Practical:	Well, what's this fellow's name?
Bolivar:	Name of Wolf. B. B. Wolf. Says he wants a job.
Practical:	Well, show him in. *(very brusque and abrupt)* Yes, Mr. Wolf, what do you want? I don't have much time—out with it. What do you do? Are you a finish carpenter? A floor man? Insulation? Roof? What's your game?
Wolf:	*(proudly)* Well, actually, I'm a huffer-puffer.
Practical:	*(laughing)* A huffer-puffer! What in the world is that? Now I've heard everything! A huffer-puffer!
Wolf:	*(self-consciously)* Well, it's a . . . well, you know the wind? Well, uh . . .
Practical:	Okay, okay. Look, I haven't got a lot of time, huh? Why don't you give a demonstration?
Wolf:	Right here? Well, okay. *(Removes coat and fangs, winds up and blows.)*
Practical:	Whew! You could use some mouthwash. By the way, did you take a shower this morning?
Wolf:	*(worried)* Why? Is there one missing? Look, Mr. Pig, you've got to hire me or I'll huff and I'll puff and I'll blow your house down.
Practical:	Look, Wolf, I don't need a huffer-puffer, and I can't even use you for air conditioning. So why don't you just *(hah-hah)* blow?
Wolf:	Gladly. *(Blows on Practical.)*
Practical:	Not on me, you idiot! Get lost—leave!
Wolf:	*(Goes off dejectedly.)* Oh, I'm just a failure. I think I'll go commit suicide. I'll put my nose in my ear and blow my brains out. I'll swallow a thermometer so I can die by degrees. Life is not worth living. *(Exits.)*
Practical:	Now, men, Let me see those plans for the United Nations Building. Hmmm—no—no—no! I don't care if you do want to be sheltered from the rain, how many times do I have to tell you? You can't start on the second floor. Get out! Get out—you're all idiots!

THIS IS YOUR KNIFE

Here's a crazy little skit that's a takeoff on the old TV show, "This is Your Life." Five characters are needed: the announcer, the emcee, Mr. Gang Green, Aunt Jemima, and the teacher.

Announcer: Welcome to the program "This is Your Knife." And now our Master of Ceremonies, Rig R. Mortis.

MC: Good evening, ladies and gentlemen! Tonight we have a very special guest, but first a word from our sponsor, Casey's Coffins.

Announcer: Casey Coffins, they are fine,
Made of satin, brass, and pine.
When you're going to pass away,
Always go the Casey way.

   The Casey Coffin Company is happy to announce a new contest. All who expect to go at one time or another are eligible to enter this contest. Simply complete the following sentence in twenty-five words or less—"I would like to go in a Casey Coffin because . . ." Send your entry to The Casey Coffin Company Contest, Casey Coffins, Inc., Land-U-Lack, Michigan.

   First prize to the lucky winner will be the new Casey creation especially designed to enhance your going and to make your long stay comfortable—the new, all new, Casey Asbestos Coffin.

   And kids, don't forget to get your Casey Coffin Badge. Just tear two tops off box cars and mail to Casey Coffins, Inc., Land-U-Lack, Michigan. And when you get your Casey Coffin Badge, the kids on your block will say "Dig that, man!"

MC: And now, ladies and gentlemen, our special guest of the evening, the local Mortician, Mr. Gang Green. Good evening, Mr. Green—how are things down at the mortuary?

Green: Dead.

MC:	I mean, how is business?
Green:	Actually, it's pretty good—people are just dying to give us their business.
MC:	Mr. Green, tonight we have with us a few of your old friends, and we're anxious to bring them out. But first, please tell us a little bit about your life.
Green:	I was born at a very early age. It came as such a surprise to me that I couldn't talk for a year and a half. Besides that, I couldn't walk for a year either. When I was born my parents weren't poor, they just didn't have any money. I was actually born at home, but when my mother saw me she was taken to the hospital. She spent three years trying to find a loophole in my birth certificate. When I was born they didn't know who to tell first—my father or Ripley. My father was an electrician and I was his first shock.
MC:	And now, Mr. Green, you're going to hear a famous voice out of your past. Can you tell us who it is?
Aunt:	Do you remember the time I came home and caught you sitting in the living room in front of a roaring fire?
MC:	Do you recognize that voice out of your past, Mr. Green?
Green:	I sure do, that's my old Aunt who raised me from a baby. Aunt Jemima, how are you?
MC:	That's right, it's your dear Aunt Jemima, and now please finish your story, Aunty.
Aunt:	I came home from shopping one day, and I found dear little Gangy sitting there in the middle of the living room in front of a blazing fire. Well, I was quite angry because there was no fireplace in our home—I was really burned up. He was a bright child, though. His parents nearly named him Coffee because he kept them awake at night.
MC:	What did Mr. Green's parents do for a living?
Aunt:	They are in the iron and steel business—his mother irons and his father steals. They had a very hard life, and they could not afford to buy Gangy shoes. They had to paint his feet black and lace up his toes.
MC:	Thanks so much for your time, Aunty. Now, Mr. Green, tell us about your school life.
Green:	Well, I was always getting blamed for things I didn't do . . . like arithmetic, reading, spelling, and history. I remember one of my teachers—he was so cross

eyed, he couldn't control his pupils. He was so cross eyed that when he cried, the tears rolled down his back—had to go to the hospital seven times for bacteria.

MC: Now, Mr. Green, listen to the next voice from your past!

Teacher: Remember how you used to keep me on my toes by putting tacks on my chair?

MC: Recognize that voice from your past, Mr. Green?

Green: Why, ah, yes—that sounds like my teacher that I thought so much of.

MC: Yes, that's right, your sixth-grade teacher. In fact I think it's the same one you referred to earlier in the program.

Green: *(embarrassed)* Yes.

Teacher: I remember when Green graduated from sixth grade. He forgot to shave that day. He was in that grade so long that the students thought *he* was the teacher.

MC: Didn't you follow Mr. Green's progress as he graduated from high school and went on to college?

Teacher: Yes, I was curious to see if Green could manage to stay in college, so I kept in contact with him. I heard that he was studying to be a bone specialist. I always said he had the head for it.

MC: Thank you so much. I know Mr. Green truly cherishes these memories. You're something of a poet, aren't you, Mr. Green?

Green: Knowing I was going to be on your show, I composed this little poem just for the occasion:

    TB or not TB, that is congestion
    Consumption be done about it?
    Of Corpse! Of Corpse!
    But it will take a lung, lung time.

MC: Thank you Mr. Green, it was a real pleasure to have you on our program! Now a closing word from our sponsor!

Announcer: Casey Coffins, they are fine
Made of satin, brass, and pine
If you want to surprise your sweeter,
Get her one that's made of cedar.
    Tune in again next week for another "This is Your Knife."
    Our guest then will be Mr. Ima Stiff.

WITCH SKIT

This skit requires two guys. One is dressed up like a witch, with the usual witchy apparel: a black hat and dress, long crooked nose, scraggly wig (an old mop will do), and a broom. The other guy is an average but good-looking young man who is extremely depressed and is about to commit suicide. As the skit begins, we find him ready to end it all . . .

Man: I can't take it any longer! I've lost my family, my job, my friends, and my house burned down. Life isn't worth living! I'm going to end it all right now . . . *(and on and on, ad lib)*

Witch: *(Enters, speaks in a squeaky voice.)* What are you doing, young man? Ha-ha-ha-hee-hee-hee *(and other witch-like sounds)*.

Man: I've lost everything. Now I'm going to jump off this cliff and end it all.

Witch: Oh, no, don't do that.

Man: Why shouldn't I?

Witch: Because, tee-hee, I'm a witch with magic powers and I can give you back everything you lost and more! I'll grant you three wishes! Tee-hee-hee! Three wishes!

Man: You mean you can give me three wishes? Wow—I wouldn't have to end it all! Hey, wait a minute. How do I know you're telling me the truth? How do I know you really are a witch?

Witch:	Of course I'm a witch. Don't I *look* like a witch? Ha-ha-ha-hee-hee-hee. I'll give you your three wishes in exchange for one small favor.
Man:	One favor? *(skeptical)* I knew there must be a catch. What do you want from me?
Witch:	Three kisses. It's a fair exchange. Three wishes for three kisses!
Man:	I think I'll just jump anyway.
Witch:	Think of all you'll be able to wish for in three wishes!
Man:	*(He finally decides to go ahead with it, so he takes the witch in his arms and begins to kiss her. After each kiss, he makes disgusted gestures, spitting each time. The last kiss bothers him especially, and after it he gives a great sigh of relief. The witch, on the other hand, shows extreme enjoyment with each kiss, smiling and making squeals of pleasure each time.)* Okay, now that that's over, I want my three wishes.
Witch:	First of all, tell me how old you are, sonny.
Man:	*(He tells her his age.)*
Witch:	And you still believe in witches at that age? Ha-ha-ha-hee-hee-hee . . . *(She exits, cackling to herself.)*

CHAPTER TWO

SLAPSTICK SKITS
AND
SIGHT GAGS

ALVIN AWARDS

There's nothing like a good pie fight for laughs. This skit turns into that, but it begins as something else entirely, taking the audience completely off guard. This skit works best at a camp or a large rally-type gathering.

Announce that Mr. and Mrs. J. P. Alvin (or anyone, for that matter) have given a special trophy to be awarded to the "outstanding young person" of the year. Make a big deal about how the winner was chosen for hard work, honesty, character, and so forth. Then, announce the winner and allow the audience to applaud. So far, everything should be done with dignity and respect.

The winner should be a girl, who is in on the joke. She should have dressed up ahead of time in a nice dress in honor of the occasion. She comes forward to receive her award, which is visible on the table—a large trophy (that you have borrowed for the evening).

When everyone is set, you say "And now, we would like to present the first annual J. P. Alvin award. . . ." You reach for the trophy, but instead, pick up a shaving cream or whipped cream pie that is hidden behind the trophy, or under the table. You smack the girl right in the face with it. She expects it, of course, but acts surprised and shocked. You laugh like the whole thing was a big joke, and the girl picks up another pie from under the table and hits you with it. You pick up another pie and hit her with it, and so on. The girl's boyfriend can also get into the act by bringing up a pie or two of his own and letting you have it. A "free-for-all" develops—and the kids love the wacky humor of it all.

As many people as you want can get involved, but you should be careful not to let it get out of control.

AND THE LAMP WENT OUT

This skit is essentially a series of over fifty sight gags that accompany a script read by a narrator. There are four actors required, besides the narrator: Evelyn DeVere (the heroine), Ralph Grayson (the hero), Mrs. DeVere (Evelyn's mother), and the evil Herbert Vanderslice (the villain). The setting is in the library of the DeVere home.

As the narrator reads the script below, the characters or the stagehands perform the actions called for at each numbered footnote in the script. (The corresponding actions are listed following the script.) Ham acting is essential in order to make the skit as ridiculous as possible. This skit works best on a formal stage with curtains.

The following props are necessary:

Onstage:

false arm to fit under Mother's sweater or dress sleeve
small pail
small sponge filled with water concealed in handkerchief
whisk broom
traveling bag or briefcase
large clock
calendar
thermometer
photograph
needlework for Mother
lamp to "go out"

Offstage:

broom
pans or drums for thunder
branches of tree to wave
moon made of tin or cardboard covered with foil
comic book for Evelyn
strong flashlight
red paper heart for Ralph
chains
sign with "time" written on it

The Script (to be read by the narrator):

Fiercely the storm raged—the rain fell in torrents, the trees were lashed by the fury of the elements,[1] the thunder crashed and roared.[2] But within the softly lighted library, silence reigned. Presently the door opened and Evelyn DeVere tripped into the room.[3] Gracefully sinking into a chair, she was soon engrossed in the latest novel of the day.[4]

Footsteps were heard,[5] and tossing her book aside,[6] Evelyn sprang to meet the newcomer.[7] But disappointment was written plainly on her face when Herbert Vanderslice stepped over the threshold.[8] Although it was not he whom she had expected, she greeted him pleasantly.[9]

The young Vanderslice's nervousness was evident.[10] He paced the floor rapidly for a moment,[11] then dropped to his knees at Evelyn's side[12] and, clasping her hand in his, cried, "Evelyn, pride of my heart, I love you. I cannot live without you. Say that you will be mine and make me the happiest man in the world."[13]

Evelyn answered, "Herbert, I cannot. I am sorry for your sake that it cannot be, but I do not love you." Withdrawing her hand from his, she rose and, walking to the table, gazed lovingly at the framed photograph there.[14]

Springing to his feet,[15] Herbert cried, "Aha! I see it all now. You love Ralph Grayson—but I swear you shall never be his."

Evelyn was greatly frightened by his manner, and her tears fell fast.[16] Herbert, turning, saw Mrs. DeVere standing in the doorway. Giving him a look of scorn, she swept into the room.[17]

"So you threaten my child—you cad, you scoundrel!" she cried. "Leave this house and never darken our doors again."[18] Bewildered at her wrath, he stood, nailed to the spot.[19] Time passed rapidly;[20] still he did not move. Then Evelyn, with never a glance in his direction, took her mother's arm and left the room.[21]

"Go!" said Mrs. DeVere. Herbert attempted to speak, but she silenced him with a gesture. Just then the clock struck.[22] Vanderslice staggered through the doorway.

Weeks flew by.[23]

It was a beautiful night; the moon rose[24] and its silvery beams played about the room.[25] Mrs. DeVere was sitting in the library, doing a dainty bit of punchwork,[26] the picture of placid industry, when a hearty laugh was heard, and Ralph Grayson slid into the room.[27]

Dropping her work[28] with a glad cry of welcome, she rose to meet him with outstretched arms.[29] "Ralph, my dear boy, I am so glad to see you! When did you return? We have missed you sorely during your travels."

"And where is she to whom my heart belongs?" said young Grayson excitedly.[30]

Mrs. DeVere pointed to the conservatory and, smiling, said, "You will find her there."[31]

Evelyn's mother, memories crowding, sat thoughtfully, but was startled by the sounds of someone creeping softly into the room.[32] Startled to see that it was Herbert Vanderslice, she rose from her chair, and drawing herself to her full majestic height, said in a haughty manner, "Pray, to what do I owe this unexpected intrusion? Have I not forbidden you in the house?"[33]

"Mrs. DeVere, I must and shall see Evelyn, and naught can . . ." Just then the door opened and Evelyn and Ralph danced gaily in,[34] smiling and happy. When Evelyn saw Herbert there, she turned a little pale.[35] "Did you wish to see me?" she asked.

In the midst of the warmth and light, he shivered, chilled by the frosty tones of her voice,[36] then frowned blackly, and striding toward her, attempted to pass Ralph. But Grayson quickly stepped forward and placed himself as a barrier between them, while Mrs. DeVere whisked her daughter from the room.[37]

Herbert in his great anger strode back and forth tearing his hair.[38] The room seemed intensely hot, and the thermometer rose rapidly.[39] Evelyn, watching the scene from the doorway, caught her breath with fear.[40] Ralph emitted a low whistle[41] as he gazed upon the insane fury of Herbert. Then, hoping to soothe the man, placed his hand on his shoulder,[42] but Herbert turned upon Ralph suddenly and the two grappled in fierce embrace.

Evelyn stood chained to the spot,[43] watching the terrific combat, but finally as Ralph threw Herbert to the floor, she ran to him with a piercing scream[44] and fell fainting at his feet.[45]

Herbert slowly picked himself up from the floor and stood quiet and subdued while they tenderly placed Evelyn in a chair.[46] Mrs. DeVere glared at him and said, "Now, young man, the tables are turned."[47] Evelyn soon revived and gazed scornfully at her rejected suitor.[48] Ralph walked to Herbert with outstretched hands and said, "Vanderslice, take your defeat like a man. I have won Evelyn, and you have lost her, but won't you wish us well?" Herbert stood motionless for a moment, then slowly extended his hand, which Ralph clasped with a hearty grip.[49] Walking to Evelyn, Herbert took her hand, pressed it to his lips then, with his face drawn with pain[50], walked haltingly from the room.[51]

Ralph held out his arms, and Evelyn ran into them. Mrs. DeVere laughingly gathered both in her embrace. Presently the lovers sauntered out toward the conservatory.[52] Mrs. DeVere resumed her dainty work, but—affected by the peace and quiet—soon dropped into gentle slumber.[53]

The clock ticked on. The lamp went out.[54]

Actions:

1. *Branches are waved from behind stage so as to be seen by the audience.*

2. Noise made by pan or drums.
3. Actually trips and stumbles.
4. Sprawls in chair and reads comic book.
5. Loud footsteps in uneven time.
6. Throws book high in air over shoulder.
7. Actually jumps.
8. Steps as if over high obstacle.
9. They shake hands. Evelyn goes back to chair.
10. Jerks and acts nervous.
11. Walking as if measuring floor.
12. Drops on knees and acts dramatically.
13. Acts as if talking.
14. Herbert follows Evelyn still on his knees.
15. Jumps up.
16. Squeezes sponge in handkerchief held to her eyes.
17. Sweeps in with broom, places it behind sofa.
18. Points dramatically to door.
19. Hammering offstage.
20. Kid with "TIME" sign runs across stage.
21. Mother holds false arm under real one. Evelyn takes it.
22. Mrs. DeVere strikes Herbert with clock.
23. Mother tears three or four leaves from calendar.
24. Moon (cardboard) is on floor at back. String attached goes over back curtain. Stagehand back of curtain pulls it up.
25. Flashlight.
26. Punches with great force into black curtain.
27. Slides as if on ice.
28. Drops work, makes noise.
29. Ralph and Mrs. DeVere shake hands.
30. Ralph takes out red paper heart. Have in back pocket. Look for it first.
31. Mother sits; Ralph exits.
32. Creep in on hands and knees.
33. Both stand up.

34. *Evelyn and Ralph waltz in together to center stage.*
35. *Lifts pail concealed behind sofa, turns it, replaces it.*
36. *Shivers and blows on hands to warm them.*
37. *Use whisk broom.*
38. *Pulls out locks of false hair.*
39. *Thermometer (large cardboard) pulled up same as moon.*
40. *Catches with hands.*
41. *Shrill whistle offstage.*
42. *Takes left hand with right, places it on Herbert's shoulder.*
43. *Chains clank. Ralph assists Herbert to lie down on floor.*
44. *Make any hideous noise offstage.*
45. *Evelyn slowly and carefully seats herself at Ralph's feet, arranges her dress, fixes hair, then lies on floor.*
46. *Ralph and Mrs. DeVere lead her to a chair.*
47. *Ralph and Mother turn end table completely around.*
48. *Very dramatic!*
49. *Use briefcase concealed behind sofa.*
50. *Makes hideous face.*
51. *Two steps, halt, repeat.*
52. *Done extravagantly.*
53. *Loud snores from behind stage.*
54. *Lamp should be securely fastened to small table draped with a long cover, under which a person is concealed. Or table and lamp can be pulled off by means of strong string.*

THE ART SHOW

Have pictures or paintings hung on a wall at different heights. Have several kids file by the pictures, stopping at each one to look for a moment or to comment to someone about the pictures. All should be dressed in raincoats or overcoats. The final kid comes by inside an overcoat which he holds over his head on a coat hanger. A hat is placed over the hanger's hook. As he reaches each picture he "adjusts his height" by raising or lowering the coat. The effect is hysterical.

AUNT BESSIE WENT TO MARKET

This crazy skit requires four or five kids who can really ham it up good. The leader brings these participants up to the front of the room and they stand in a single line, facing the audience (shoulder to shoulder).

The leader explains the "game" to the group. The leader begins by announcing to the person standing next to him (person #1) that "Aunt Bessie went to market." At this point, person #1 is to reply "Oh, really? What did she buy?" The leader responds by saying "A rocking chair." When he says "rocking chair," he begins "rocking" back and forth as if he were in a rocking chair, and he continues doing this throughout the game.

Person #1 then turns to the person on the other side of him (person #2) and says "Aunt Bessie went to market," and the whole scenario repeats itself. Now there are two people "rocking." Person #2 repeats the same sequence with person #3, and so on, to the end of the line. When everyone is finished, all of the participants, including the leader, are "rocking" back and forth.

Now the leader says again to person #1 "Aunt Bessie went to market," and again, person #1 asks "Oh, really, what did she buy?" This time he says "A bicycle," pedaling his feet while still continuing to "rock" back and forth. Person #1 repeats this with person #2, and so on down the line. Now everyone is rocking back and forth, *and* pedaling their feet. It is starting to really look ridiculous.

The leader starts the whole thing all over again, adding things like "A pogo stick," "A cuckoo clock," and other items—each time adding the appropriate motions or sounds. It is hilarious to watch all the participants trying to keep all these things going all at once. They begin to dread asking the question "Oh, really, what did she buy?"

The leader's final response to the question can be "Nothing. She died," upon which everything stops.

BANDAGED HAND ANNOUNCEMENT

This is always great at camps or larger meetings. Simply walk to the front of the group with a serious look on your face and make the following announcement. Be as convincing as you possibly can.

"I'm sorry to have to put a damper on the meeting, but I have a very important announcement to make. A few moments ago, one of the girls in our group went home. One of the guys here . . . and I won't mention his name . . . did a very crude and insensitive thing to her. While she was sitting on the bench outside, minding her own business, he approached her and very rudely tried to kiss her. He was trying to be smart, I suppose, but the girl reacted negatively and was deeply offended. When the guy tried it a second time, she swung at him with a pencil she had in her hand and seriously gashed his hand with it. The guy had to have his hand bandaged, and the girl left and probably will never come back to one of our meetings again. Things like this are needless and are a sign of immaturity. We cannot tolerate this kind of child's play anymore. I don't think I need to say anymore about it. . . ."

Usually you can hear a pin drop when you are finished making the announcement. All the while, you keep your hand in your pocket. After the announcement, casually take your hand out of your pocket (in plain view of everyone) and reveal your hand, bandaged up with blood stains all over it. As soon as the kids notice it, the laughs begin.

BELLY-WHISTLE

Announce that you have invited a great new talent to your meeting, Mr. Tummy Tootwhistle, to perform a musical number. Mr. Tootwhistle comes out wearing a giant hat that covers his head, arms, and shoulders, and he has a shirt and bow tie at his waist, with fake arms hanging from his hips. Painted on the guy's bare stomach is a face, with the mouth being his navel, giving the appearance that the mouth is in a "puckered" or whistling position. The guy then whistles a tune, making his stomach go in and out, which looks like puffing cheeks. A tape recording of the whistling can be used if the guy can't whistle very good. This is hysterical to watch and provides a lot of laughs in a meeting.

THE CANDY STORE

Four guys enter the "candy store," which is run by an old man (bent over, shaky voice, beard and cane). First guy asks for a dime's worth of jelly beans. Old man notices that the jelly beans are on the top shelf and tries to talk him out of it, but the guy insists. So the old man gets a ladder and with much pain climbs to the top, gets the jelly beans and comes down the ladder. He puts the ladder away. The second guy does the same thing and asks for a dime's worth of jelly beans. Again the old man goes through the same bit, and gets him the jelly beans. After he does, the third guy also asks for a dime's worth of jelly beans and the very annoyed and tired old man climbs up his ladder again getting the jelly beans. This time while he is up there, he asks the last guy, "I suppose you want a dime's worth of jelly beans too?" The last guy says "No." The old man comes down and puts the ladder away again. "Now, what do you want?" he asks. The guy answers, "I want a nickel's worth of jelly beans." The old man chases him out of the store with his cane, shouting.

A DAY IN THE DESERT

Place a glass of water in the middle of the floor, with a sign that says "Oasis." Three guys crawl in, crying out "Water, water, we've got to have some water!" Two of the guys die before making it to the water, but the third finally reaches the glass. He picks up the glass of water, pulls out his comb, dips it in the water, and walks away happily combing his hair.

DARLING DAINTY DOTTY

Here's a classic old-time melodrama, with plenty of room for slapstick acting and some outrageous sight gags.

Characters:

Lester Longfoot, the Uncle
Lucretia Longfoot, the Aunt
Sly Sylvester Smythe, the greedy landlord
Dainty Dotty Dudley, the heroine
Plain Peter Porter, the hero
The narrator

The scene is the humble home of Uncle Lester Longfoot. There is a table on the stage with plain chairs around it. There are a few dishes on the table. Behind the dishes are a flat iron, a hammer, and a bicycle pump. There is a large chair at the left. A folding screen can be used for the back of the room. There is a large calendar on the screen along with pictures, if desired. As the scene opens, Uncle Lester is in the big chair reading. Aunt Lucretia sits at the table mending a long black stocking. There is a brick hidden inside the stocking.

Uncle Lester:	*(looking up)* Where is our niece, Dainty Dotty?
Aunt Lucretia:	Getting ready for her sweetheart. He is coming by tonight.
Uncle Lester:	You mean our neighbor, handsome Peter Porter?
Aunt Lucretia:	Ah, he is handsome! *(Sighs.)* But he wants to be called just Plain Peter.
Uncle Lester:	I hope he remembers that deep dark ditch by the door. I must fix that some day. *(Enter Dainty Dotty, taking tiny steps. She walks over to the table.)*
Dainty Dotty:	How do I look, Aunt Lucretia?
Aunt Lucretia:	Plain Peter Porter will lose his heart. *(Loud rap is heard.)*
Dainty Dotty:	There he is now! *(Uncle goes to door.)*
Narrator:	But alas! It was not Plain Peter Porter. It was the evil Sly Sylvester Smythe, the greedy landlord. Could it be that the mortgage was due? *(Uncle steps back. Aunt leaps up and drops the stocking with the brick onto the floor. Dainty Dotty flutters her eyes.)*

Sylvester:	(taking big steps into the room) I'm here to see your niece, Dainty Dotty. (Twirls mustache.)
Dainty Dotty:	But sir! I am expecting another!
Sylvester:	Aha, my pretty! Would it be Plain Peter Porter?
Narrator:	Dainty Dotty turned shyly away, and dropped her eyes to the floor. (Dainty Dotty holds two golf balls hidden in handkerchief to face, then lets them drop onto the floor.)
Sylvester:	I offer you riches! (He pulls out a huge cloth bag marked with a dollar sign.)
Dainty Dotty:	Nay! Nay! (Sobs.)
Sylvester:	And a big house!
Dainty Dotty:	Nay! Nay! (Sobs.)
Sylvester:	Very well, my pretty! The mortgage is due! (He pulls out a long paper and lets its end fall to the floor.) Heh-heh! But marry me, and I will forget this!
Dainty Dotty:	Nay! Nay! Never!
Narrator:	Then, holding her head high, she gave him the air! (Dainty Dotty grabs the bicycle pump and pumps air toward Sylvester.)
Sylvester:	(stepping back) You will hear from me, my pretty! (He exits, shaking his fist. The aunt sobs. The uncle comforts her. Dainty Dotty flutters her eyes.)
Narrator:	There was another knock at the door. (knocks) It was Plain Peter Porter! (Enter Plain Peter, flexing his muscles.)
Plain Peter:	What is the matter, my darling Dainty Dotty?
Dainty Dotty:	(sobbing) Oh, Plain Peter! The mortgage is due! We will lose our home unless I marry Sly Sylvester Smythe at once!
Plain Peter:	Never! The cad! I will get him with one bare hand! (He pulls back his sleeve and shows the likeness of a bear's paw—a stuffed brown mitten with cardboard claws.)
Dainty Dotty:	My hero!
Narrator:	Plain Peter Porter pressed her hand. (Plain Peter picks up the flat iron, puts her hand on the table and presses it.)
Plain Peter:	I fly away to save thee! (Flaps arms and circles around the room, then exits. Dainty Dotty sighs, and falls into the chair.)

Narrator:	The days flew by. *(Uncle goes to the calendar and tears off several pages. Footsteps are heard outside.)*
Aunt Lucretia:	That must be Plain Peter Porter!
Uncle Lester:	I hope he remembered the deep dark ditch by the door. I must fix that some day.
Narrator:	But alas! It was not Plain Peter Porter! It was Sly Sylvester Smythe, the greedy landlord!
Sylvester:	I have come for Dainty Dotty! Or to foreclose!
Dainty Dotty:	*(reentering the room)* Is it Plain Peter Porter?
Sylvester:	I have come for you, my pretty! *(Twirls mustache.)* Or I foreclose!
Narrator:	Uncle Lester tore his hair! *(Uncle pulls loose yarn scraps from his hair.)*
Narrator:	Dainty Dotty's tears came down like rain! *(Dainty Dotty sobs into a handkerchief containing a waterfilled sponge.)*
Narrator:	A chill as of winter filled the room! *(Handfuls of "snow" are tossed over the screen.)*
Sylvester:	What do you say now, my pretty? Heh-heh!
Dainty Dotty:	*(bowing her head)* Uncle Lester, give him my hand in marriage. *(Sobs.)* There is no other way. *(Dotty pulls a stuffed pink glove from her pocket and hands it to Uncle.)*
Narrator:	Uncle Lester beat his chest in despair. *(Uncle picks up the hammer and pounds his chest. Drum beats offstage.)*
Narrator:	Aunt Lucretia threw her arms onto the table, sobbing wildly. *(Aunt pulls stuffed "arms" from big sleeves, and throws them onto the table.)*
Plain Peter:	*(rushing in)* Take the hand of Dainty Dotty, would you? *(Flexes muscles and grabs Sylvester. Their faces touch as they glare at each other.)*
Plain Peter:	How about a sock on the nose! *(Pulls out a long sock and slaps Sylvester on the nose with it.)* And how about a big black eye! *(Pulls out a huge letter "I" cut from black cardboard.)*
Sylvester:	No, not that! *(He drops the mortgage on the floor and leaps out the door. Plain Peter gallops after him.)*
Uncle Lester:	Plain Peter! Don't forget about that . . . *(There is a loud crashing noise outside.)* deep dark ditch by the door!

Narrator:	It was very quiet for a moment. Then . . . footsteps. *(Plain Peter limps back into the room.)*
Plain Peter:	Look what I found in the deep dark ditch by the door! *(He holds up a rock.)*
Uncle Lester:	Why, it's GOLD! GOLD!
Aunt Lucretia:	*(jumping up and down)* Gold! We're rich!
Uncle Lester:	We can pay off the mortgage!
Plain Peter:	Oh, my darling Dainty Dotty! We can be wed! *(Plain Peter and Dainty Dotty hold hands and skip around the room and exit. Uncle and Aunt sit at the table.)*
Aunt Lucretia:	Oh, I am so happy! *(sniffing)* I could just cry! *(She pulls out a large handkerchief and sobs loudly.)*
Narrator:	And Uncle Lester was happy too. *(Uncle takes the other end of the handkerchief and blows his nose. A horn blasts offstage. There is a pause.)* It was very still. *(Uncle and Aunt lean back in their chairs and begin to snore.)* The sun went down. *(pause)* The moon rose. *(A cardboard moon on a stick is raised from the back of the screen.)* And night fell. *(There is a great thump offstage.)*

THE DOCTOR'S OFFICE

The scene for this skit is the waiting room of a doctor's office. There are a few chairs and magazines in the room, and there is a receptionist seated at a table.

The first patient of the day enters and says to the receptionist, "I'm Mr. Smith. I have an appointment." She replies, "Fine. Please have a seat."

The next patient enters and says to the receptionist, "I'm Mr. Frick. I have an appointment." The receptionist replies, "Fine. Please have a seat," and Frick does. All the while, Frick is jerking his head violently (sideways) every four or five seconds and Smith watches. This continues for a while, and suddenly Smith starts uncontrollably jerking his head in the same manner as Frick. Meanwhile Frick's head stops jerking and Smith's head continues to jerk. Frick feels his neck, and says with a big smile, "Hey, my problem is gone! Cancel my appointment!" He leaves.

Smith continues to jerk his head.

The next patient, Mr. Ferd, says the same thing to the receptionist, sits down, and begins flinging his arm in front of his chest in a spastic fashion. Smith, still jerking his head, notices Ferd's apparent problem, and pretty soon starts flinging his arm the same as Ferd. Now he is both flinging his arm, and jerking his head, and Ferd's arm stops. Ferd smiles and says, "Wow! My problem is gone! Cancel my appointment." He leaves.

Smith, with a look of real puzzlement on his face, continues to jerk his head and fling his arm.

The next several patients enter, one at a time, and the same thing occurs each time. One man has a leg that keeps kicking out in front of him, and Smith catches his problem and starts kicking his leg, too. Another man comes in snapping his fingers, and Smith winds up snapping his fingers. Each time, Smith catches the new "disease," and the person who originally had it is miraculously cured. At this point, Smith should be jerking his head, flinging his arm, kicking his leg, snapping his fingers, and so on.

The last patient to enter is a pregnant lady. Smith notices her as she comes in, and with horror on his face, he screams and runs out of the doctor's office.

THE ENLARGING MACHINE

For this skit you need a large refrigerator box with a hole in it and with dials, knobs, and meters painted on like a computer. Inside the box, concealed from the audience, is a helper. (No one should know about him.)

The creator of the machine, Dr. Einsteinski, demonstrates—he throws a handkerchief into the hole and out comes a sheet; in goes a piece of string, out comes a rope; in goes a ping-pong ball, out comes a basketball. Applause follows each demonstration. A "lady" then walks by carrying a baby (doll). Just as she gets in front of the machine, she trips and accidentally tosses the baby into the machine. The scientist yells, "Oh, no!" and out of the machine busts the "helper," a big guy in diapers with a bottle, shouting, "Mommy!"

AN EVENING WITH GRANDMA

Here is another spoof on melodramas using a series of sight gags similar to "And the Lamp Went Out." It requires no acting ability at all. The narrator simply reads the script, and the characters do as they are instructed in the "actions" following the script. The hard part is getting together all the props you need, but most of them are easy to find. Encourage the characters to really ham it up and have fun. It is guaranteed to be a winner, especially at camps and conferences.

The Characters:

Manuel—should be dressed in black
Maggie—should be dressed in old-fashioned dress
Patrick—should be in white
Zingerella—dressed like a housekeeper
Two people to be the "curtains" (They hold signs to that effect.)
Two people to be the "hours" (They also have signs.)
The sun (boy or girl)
Night (boy or girl)
The narrator

Props Needed:

pitcher of water	large wooden match
a podium	notes
chalk	signs (below):
trading or postage stamps	curtains (2)
broom	stairs
pail (bucket)	time
banana	no (30 or more)
police whistle	hours (2)
iron	sun
rope	night
salt shakers (2)	

The Script: To be read by the narrator as the characters act according to instructions given in the footnotes.

The curtains part.[1]

The sun rises.[2]

Our play begins.

Manuel de Populo, son of a wealthy merchant, is in his study, carefully poring over his notes.[3] He stamps his feet[4] impatiently, and calls for his maid, Zingerella.

Zingerella tears down the stairs[5] and trips into the room.[6] "Go fetch Maggie O'Toole," demands Manuel. Zingerella flies[7] to do her master's bidding.

Time passes.[8]

Manuel crosses the floor—once—twice—thrice.[9] At last Maggie comes sweeping into the room.[20]

"For the last time, will you marry me?" insists Manuel. Maggie turns a little pale.[11]

"NO," she shouts, "A thousand times NO."[12]

"Then I will have to cast you into the dungeon," says Manuel, in a rage.

She throws herself at his feet.[13] "Oh, sir," she pleads, "I appeal to you."[14]

Haughtily he says, "Your appeal is fruitless,"[15] and stomps out of the room.[16]

Maggie flies about in a dither.[17] Oh, if only Patrick would come—*he* would save her! The hours pass slowly.[18] Finally Maggie takes her stand,[19] and scans[20] the horizon. Suddenly she hears a whistle.[21] Could it be . . . ?

"Maggie, it is I, my love, your Patrick!"

He enters the room and tenderly presses her hand.[22] She throws him a line.[23] Just at that moment; Manuel reenters and challenges Patrick to a duel. In a fury, they assault each other.[24] Finally Manuel gives up the match[25] and departs. "At last, you are mine!" says Patrick. He leads his love away into the night.[26] The sun sets.[27] Night falls.[28] The curtains come together[29] and our play is ended.

Actions:

1. Two people with signs that say "curtains" walk away from each other, beginning at center of the stage.
2. Person with "sun" sign stands up.
3. He pours water from a pitcher all over some notes.
4. Licks stamps, sticks on shoes.
5. Rips down a sign that says "stairs" and tears it up.
6. Falls down (trips).

7. Waves arms in flying motion.
8. Guy holding "time" sign walks across stage.
9. Takes chalk and makes three big "X's" on the floor.
10. Sweeps with a broom.
11. Turns a pail upside down.
12. Throws papers with "no" on them.
13. Falls at his feet and lies there.
14. Hands him a banana peel.
15. Hands the banana peel back.
16. Stomps his feet.
17. Waves arms in flying manner.
18. Two people with "hours" signs walk across the stage.
19. Stands behind podium.
20. Hand above eyes in searching motion.
21. Patrick blows police whistle.
22. Takes iron and irons her hand.
23. Throws a rope at him.
24. Take salt shakers and sprinkle each other.
25. Hands Patrick a wooden match.
26. Bump into the guy with the "night" sign.
27. "Sun" sits down.
28. "Night" falls down.
29. "Curtains" walk toward each other.

FAMILY FOLLIES

A great skit idea is to (secretly) have members of your youth group research the family life of a family in your church. Then, prepare a skit called, "A Day in the Life of the (Joneses)." Someone plays the father, mother, brothers and sister, and it begins with everybody waking up and going through a typical day (maybe Sunday). Because the skit is about people that everybody knows, it will get a lot of laughs an ordinary skit might not get. Try putting it on for the whole church at a social.

FASHION FOLLIES

A crazy fashion show always makes a great skit if it's done with a little creativity. The following ideas work great when you set up the stage for a fashion show, with a good announcer to describe the fashions and good "fashion models" (boys or girls) who try to walk and wiggle like real models. The results can really be funny. Use these or think of some of your own:

1. *Sack dress:* dress made of a potato sack, with more paper sacks hung all over it. Maybe even a sack over the model's head.
2. *Dinner dress:* dress with menus, napkins, salt and pepper shakers, plates, food, and so on hanging all over it.
3. *Spring-flowered dress:* dress with real flowers and springs all over it. Purse can be a bucket with fertilizer and tools.
4. *Tea dress:* dress with tea bags all over it, and a teapot handbag.

5. *Multicolored skirt and scatter-pin sweater:* skirt with crayons and coloring book pictures all over it; the sweater has dozens of safety pins or ball-point pens all over it.

6. *Buckskin jacket and quilted skirt:* dollar bills pinned on jacket; a quilted bedspread made into a skirt.

7. *Slip-on sweater with matched pants:* sweater with a slip over it and pants with matchbooks all over.

8. *TV jacket (for men):* robe with *TV Guides* and antennas all over it.

9. *Smoking jacket:* Get a smoke bomb to release under the coat so smoke comes out the sleeves and collar.

10. *Brush-denim jacket:* denim jacket with brushes sewn onto it.

11. *Popcorn-weave sweater:* sweater with popcorn attached.

12. *Checkered skirt:* plastic checkers sewn onto skirt.

13. *Tank top:* box painted to look like a fish tank (cut a hole for the head).

14. *Pancake makeup:* real pancakes taped to one's cheeks.

15. *Lipstick:* wax lips on a big stick.

16. *Orange belt:* oranges in cellophane tied around model's waist.

17. *Bib overalls:* baby bib sewn onto jeans.

18. *Jump suit:* model jumps up and down all of the time.

19. *Saddle shoes:* ropes from feet to hands.

20. *Handbag:* make an outline of a hand on a purse.

21. *Grass skirt:* tape small packages of grass seed on a skirt.

22. *Cotton blouse:* put cotton balls on a blouse.

23. *Straw hat:* attach drinking straws to a hat.

24. *Colorful choker:* someone runs out on stage and appears to choke the model.

25. *Picture hat:* put small frames and pictures on a hat.

FRIENDLY TALKING MACHINE

This skit involves two people. One is an average, everyday guy and the other is a human-looking computer. He walks with machine-like motions, like a wind-up toy. There is a sign on him that says "Friendly Talking Machine" and a smaller one that says "Insert Coin Here," pointing to his shirt pocket. The Friendly Talking Machine enters the room, stops, and drops his head.

The average guy walks in, sees the sign, and deposits a dime in the F.T.M.'s pocket. The F.T.M. begins moving his arms up and down, lifts head, smiles, and says "Hi, there, I'm your Friendly Talking Machine. I am here to help you. . . ." The machine stops and drops his head again.

The average guy inserts another dime, and the machine starts up again: "Hi, there, I'm your Friendly Talking Machine. I am here to help you. Would you like to know how I can help you? . . ." Stops again, head drops.

Again, the average guy puts more money in, and the F.T.M. starts up again, each time going a little farther, adding a new phrase. Emphasis should be placed on the guy putting in more and more money.

Friendly Talking Machine's lines: (Each * shows where the average guy inserts another coin).

"Hi, there, I'm your Friendly Talking Machine. I am here to help you. * Would you like to know how I can help you? * You are sad and lonely. * Would you like to know how not to be sad and lonely? * You need a friend. * Would you like to know how to find a friend? * Give him lots of money, friend."

On completion of the next-to-last line, "Would you like to know how to find a friend?" the average guy inserts one last coin. Nothing happens. He taps machine, tries to find the problem. Finally he gets mad and starts to kick the machine, and the machine starts up suddenly. At the concluding line, the machine runs offstage with the average guy chasing.

THE GREAT PIANO RECITAL

This skit can be a lot of fun if you have an upright piano, a spinet piano, a good pianist, and a real good actor. Before the program, place an upright piano on stage or in front of the room with the spinet piano hidden behind it so the audience can't see it. Have the "real" pianist out of everyone's sight by the spinet piano and the "actor" at the upright piano (the actor should be a person who has no musical ability). Announce to the audience that a guest pianist is going to entertain everyone. Have the audience write their song requests on slips of paper, then collect them and give them to the "guest pianist." He will read the name of the request and then ham it up as if he were really playing it (while a "real" pianist on the spinet is actually playing). Half of the fun is that the visible pianist has to guess where the next notes will be on the keyboard—and even when they will come, especially if the "real" pianist gets a little tricky.

For added fun, substitute the following crazy song titles for the titles suggested by the audience:

1. "You broke my heart, but I broke your jaw"
2. "She was a moonshiner's daughter, but I love her still"
3. "They operated on Father and opened Mother's male"
4. "When you wore a tulip and I wore a big red rose, and we both got arrested"
5. "Let's go behind the rockpile, baby . . . we can get a little bolder there"
6. "Let me call you hinges; you are something to adore"
7. Old Arabian Ballad: "Oh, What a Bag Dad Had"
8. "Lord, send me a blonde; I'm tired of squeezing blackheads"
9. "I was riding high in the saddle till my blister broke"
10. "Red snails in my swimsuit"

THE HAMBURGER SKIT

Characters:

The Customer
The Waiter
The Cook (wearing no shirt, only a cook's apron)

Props: Table and chairs, set up like a restaurant
Plate of food, including a hamburger
A door near table leads to the "kitchen," offstage

The customer enters the restaurant and sits down. The waiter approaches the table and asks for his order.

Customer: I'll have a hamburger and a Coke.
Waiter: Thank you, sir. *(Exits to kitchen and returns with the hamburger and Coke.)* Here you are, sir. *(Waiter exits.)*
Customer: Thank you.

The customer takes the bun off the hamburger and starts to put ketchup on it. But before he does, he notices something on the hamburger patty. He looks disgusted and picks the "thing" up off the patty and calls the waiter.

Customer: Waiter! *(The waiter comes.)* Waiter, there's a *hair* on my hamburger. This is disgusting!

Waiter: I'm very sorry, sir. I'll get you another hamburger. *(He exits to kitchen and returns with another one.)* Here you are, sir.

Customer: Thank you.

Again, the customer starts to put ketchup on the hamburger and the same thing happens.

Customer: Waiter! Waiter! *(The waiter comes running.)* Look! There's a hair in this hamburger, too!

Waiter: I'm so very sorry, sir. Please allow me to get you another hamburger. I'm sure it won't happen again.

Customer: All right, but hurry it up.

The waiter returns with another hamburger, and the same thing happens. This time, the hair seems even longer and more disgusting than the others.

Customer: Waiter! *(The waiter returns.)* Look at this! I can't believe this place! I demand to speak to the cook!

Waiter: The cook?

Customer: Yes! I demand to see the cook right now!

Waiter: Very well, sir. *(Turns to kitchen, and yells.)* Hey, Buford! There's a customer out here who would like to have a few words with you!

Cook: *(The cook comes out where he can be seen, wearing his apron over his bare chest.)* Sure, right after I finish making up some more hamburger patties! *(He rolls up a ball of meat and then flattens it by mashing it under his armpit.)*

HOWDY, BUCKAROO!

If the kids in your group have a tough time memorizing lines, this skit might be perfect for them. Four characters are needed: a mechanical quick-draw cowboy dressed in full cowboy garb, two warehouse employees dressed appropriately, and a third employee. Only the mechanical quick-draw cowboy need remember any lines. They should be spoken in a mechanical manner: "Howdy, Buckaroo! So you think you can beat me, eh? Put on the holster at my feet and on the count of three, draw! Are you ready? One . . . Two . . . Three!"

The only props you will need are two gun-and-holster sets, one of which should be loaded with blanks.

The play begins with the two warehouse employees rolling (or carrying) in the mechanical slot-machine "cowboy" for storage. The extra gun-and-holster set is placed at the feet of the mechanical "cowboy." The two employees exit.

The third employee walks in and, seeing the robot, decides to try his luck. He reads the instructions printed on the chest of the mechanical man and then places a quarter in the slot. The robot winds up and gives the memorized spiel. The employee is unable to pick up the extra gun and holster set because it's trapped under the boot of the mechanical cowboy. He panics and turns to run as the robot counts to three and shoots the employee.

Not to be outdone, the employee lifts the robot's leg, pulls out the gun set and puts it on, and even practices his quick-draw skills several times. Confidently, he inserts another quarter. The message is repeated, but this time the employee's gun sticks in the holster and again he is shot.

For the final attempt, the employee pulls his gun, stands to the side and holds his gun to the robot's head, and inserts another quarter. The robot repeats the message, except that this time the mechanical cowboy winds down in the middle of "two." The employee bangs on the robot a couple of times to get him moving again, but no response. Disgusted, he takes off the gun, sets it down at the robot's feet and turns to walk off. The robot continues suddenly with the rest of the prerecorded message, says "three," and shoots the employee.

KOOKY CHOIRS

Sometimes it can be hilarious to have some nonmusical people perform a musical number that borders on the ridiculous. Here are some ideas:

1. *The Rhythm Band:* Have a few kids come out dressed up like a rock band and perform a song played on children's "rhythm band" instruments, like kazoos, slide-whistles, sandpaper blocks, rattles, and drums. It can be a riot.

2. *Bagpipes:* Divide your "musicians" into three sections. The first section sings "oh" continuously while lightly hitting their "Adam's apples" with the side of their hands. The second group sings "ad" and rhythmically pinches their noses, giving an alternately straight and nasal tone. The third group holds their noses, and to the tune of "The Campbells Are Coming," sings "da." Done correctly, this really does sound like bagpipes, provided the kids can keep from laughing.

3. *The Animal Fair:* Four or five guys come trotting in (from offstage) wearing a great assortment of odd-looking clothes and hats—the odder, the funnier. They line up in front of the audience shoulder to shoulder and begin singing in regular accentuated rhythmic beats— "hum! hum! hum! hum!"—all the while bobbing up and down.

The first one in line then begins singing the song—"I went to the animal fair. The birds and the mammals were there. The big baboon by the light of the moon was combing his auburn hair. The monkey he got drunk. He lit on the elephant's trunk. The elephant sneezed and fell on his knees, and that was the end of the monk!" Upon finishing, he continues singing the words, "The monk! the monk! the monk! the monk!" jumping up and down each time.

Then the next person in line sings "The Animal Fair," bouncing up and down to "The monk!" when he's finished. And so on down the line. Each person bounces differently. When all have finished, they're all jumping and shaking, singing "The monk! the monk!" They then bounce out of the room.

THE MAGIC BANDANNA

For this skit, you will need two guys. One is a magician, the other is his assistant. The magician should be dressed appropriately in tails and top hat. The assistant, who seems to be a klutz, never says anything, á la Harpo Marx. He only takes orders from his "boss," the magician. On the stage is a table. On top of the table is a bandanna. Also, nearby (such as under the table) is a sack lunch.

Magician: Ladies and gentlemen, today I am going to perform for you my famous vanishing bandanna trick. My assistant, Herkimer, will go to the table behind me, and do exactly as I say. And even though I will not look at Herkimer or the bandanna, I will be able to make it disappear in Herkimer's hand. *(to Herkimer)* All right, Herkimer . . . go to the table behind me. *(Herkimer goes to the table, and the magician stands in front, facing the audience, so that he cannot see the table or Herkimer.)*

Herkimer . . . please pick up the bandanna. *(Herkimer looks at the bandanna, but is distracted by the sack lunch under the table, so he picks it up and looks inside the bag. He discovers a banana. Then he looks puzzled, like he's not sure exactly what the magician asked him to pick up, so he throws the bandanna on the floor, and holds the banana instead.)*

Herkimer . . . take the bandanna in your right hand, please. *(He holds the banana in his right hand.)*

Now, Herkimer . . . fold the four corners of the bandanna together. *(Herkimer begins peeling the banana, counting one, two, three, four. He throws the peel on the floor.)*

Now stuff the bandanna into your left fist and don't let any of it show, Herkimer! *(Herkimer takes the banana and crams it into his fist, causing the squashed up banana to come oozing out between his fingers.)*

Finally, Herkimer . . . on the count of three . . . throw the bandanna up into the air, and the bandanna will be gone! ONE . . . TWO . . . THREE! *(On the count of three, Herkimer throws the mashed-up banana at the magician . . . and the magician chases Herkimer offstage.)*

THE MIDGET SKIT

This popular skit requires two people who are reasonably creative. It works best when presented on a stage with a curtain and no lighting except for a spotlight on the "midget." You'll need the following props:

table covered with a sheet or blanket
men's long-sleeved shirt
Bermuda shorts
shoes (large work shoes are best)
paper bag containing a toothbrush, a can of shaving cream, a safety razor (with no blade, please!), banana, peanut butter and jam sandwich, and cream pie
towel lying on table

The lead man of this skit should be someone who can ad-lib well. He stands behind the table with the shorts around his arms, his hands in the shoes, and the shirt buttoned around his neck. A helper stands directly behind him and puts his hands through the sleeves of the shirt.

During the course of the skit it will be necessary for the "midget" to shave, brush his teeth, eat, and so on. The arms doing all of that, of course, will belong to the helper standing behind, who won't be able to see what he's doing. The movement should all be exaggerated—smearing toothpaste all over the lead man's nose, brushing his cheeks, sticking a banana in his eye, and so on. The feet can also do some funny things, like clicking heels together or running.

You'll want to give some forethought to the lead man's monologue. One good idea is to have the "midget" hitchhiking to some event that you want to advertise. He explains to the audience where he's going and that he needs a ride. Several cars go by. Finally, one stops and the "midget" gets in (although he does not actually move anywhere). He talks to the driver of the car and explains where he is going and asks if he can shave before he gets there. After shaving, he asks if he can eat his lunch. Afterward, he brushes his teeth, gets out of the car, and thanks the driver.

The "midget" can also be a girl. Just change the costuming and supply beauty aids such as lipstick and mascara. Then have a beauty class.

The more creative and uninhibited the participants are, the more successful the skit will be.

MOTHER, I'M DYING

You'll need some extremely outgoing actors for this slapstick routine. It can be hilarious—but only if the actors take their parts to the limit. There are four "actors," plus the "director." The "actors" perform a play three times: the first time, in a boring way; the second time, as a hysterical tragedy; the third time, as a riotous comedy. Lines and actions should be mostly ad-libbed, based on this sketch.

Director: Tonight the Little Theater Guild would like to present a new avant-garde play about a provocative teenage tragedy. The characters are the daughter, the mother, the doctor, the mortician. Our scene opens with mother sitting in the living room as the teenage daughter enters with a problem.

NOTE: *The following scene is acted without any emotion—completely deadpan.*

Daughter: Mother, I think I'm dying.

Mother: Oh, thank goodness it's nothing serious. I suppose I should call the doctor. I hate to inconvenience him. *(Crosses to phone.)* Hello, doctor. Oh, I'm fine, thank you. How are you? Say, my daughter says she thinks she's dying. When you get time, could you come over and check on her?

The daughter lies down on a table. There's a knock at the door, and mother gets up to answer.

Mother: Oh, hello, doctor. Come on in. My daughter's collapsed over there. Would you like some coffee? *(He politely refuses, then crosses to daughter and bends over her, listening with stethoscope.)*

Doctor: No, your daughter's not dying . . . she's dead.

Mother: Well, how about that. Guess I'll call the mortician. *(Crosses to phone.)* Hello, mortician. Say, my daughter's dead, do you think you could come over within a few days and take care of her? O.K. Goodbye.

The mortician knocks at the door and the mother answers.

Mother:	Hello, mortician. My daughter's over there.
Mortician:	*(Measures daughter from head to toe.)* She'll fit.
Director:	*(furious)* Stop! Stop! That was terrible! That was the worst acting I've ever seen. Where was the emotion? There wasn't any! None! Now, I want you to do the whole thing over again. This time use a little emotion . . . in fact, use a *lot* of emotion!

The cast repeats the entire skit, crying hysterically. The lines do not have to be delivered exactly as before—in fact, the more creative and uninhibited the actors, the better. When the skit ends, the director again jumps to his feet and shouts:

Director:	That was horrible! What's the matter with you knuckleheads? Now you went too far with the emotion. You can't have all tears and sadness. Now, do it over again. This time use some humor. After all, even Shakespeare had humor in his tragedies.

The cast repeats the complete skit, laughing hysterically. When it's over, the director jumps up, tearing his hair, and throws them out.

NO MATTER WHAT SHAPE YOUR STOMACH'S IN

This skit takes place "inside" the human body. Set up your room so that the stage area is the stomach, the center aisle is the throat, and the door is the mouth.

Any variation of this basic set up will work. Put up signs—"Stomach," "Mouth," and so on—and any other decorations that might help get the idea across. Next you need a sound effects man, on a microphone, to make appropriate sounds as the skit progresses.

Characters:

four or five "stomach acids" (Hang signs around their necks that say "Stomach Acid.")
a taco (kid dressed in Mexican clothes)

chop suey (kid dressed in Chinese clothes)

French fries (kid wearing a beret)

hot dog (kid on all fours, barking like a dog)

chicken (kid clucking like a chicken)

or any other foods you want (costumes and behavior should be ridiculous)

As the skit begins, the stomach acids are on the stage (stomach). The sound effects man is making gurgling noises on the microphone and the stomach acids are holding their stomachs in pain, saying "Boy, am I hungry! When are we going to get something to eat?" Suddenly, one of them says, "Look! Food! Here comes a taco! Oh, boy!" The taco comes in the door (mouth) and starts down the aisle (throat). The stomach acids hide. The sound effects man begins to make more excited gurgling sounds. The taco walks into the stomach, looking around nonchalantly—suddenly the stomach acids jump out and attack the taco, beating it up and biting it. Now the sound effects man is gurgling and slurping like crazy. The taco puts up a fight, but loses, falling to the floor, and the stomach acids smile, rubbing their stomachs, saying, "Ahhh, that was delicious."

Then the chop suey enters, and they do the same thing, jumping on the chop suey and beating it up. This happens to all the food, until the stage area is covered with "eaten" food lying all over the floor. The stomach acids say, "Boy, am I full. I'm really stuffed," and they lie down to go to sleep, with the sound effects man gurgling quietly. As the stomach acids sleep, the taco slowly gets up, wakes up the chop suey and the other foods and they attack the sleeping stomach acids. They beat them up, and the sound effects man starts making vomiting noises over the microphone as the foods run down the aisle and out the door.

PING-PONG SKIT

Find two guys who can make loud "clicks" against the roof of their mouth with their tongue, a sound like a Ping-Pong ball hit with a paddle.

The two of them each hold a paddle and begin playing on an imaginary table, making the sound effects with their mouths. They gradually get farther and farther apart, making the clicks farther apart, too.

Finally, they get so far apart they disappear offstage (or exit out side doors). When they reappear, they have switched positions and walk in backwards, continuing their game; but now it looks like they are hitting the ball all the way around the world. They continue playing and walking backwards toward each other until they pass each other so that now they're facing each other again, and play a fast game as before.

THE SNEAK THIEF

Two gentlemen dressed in business suits walk into a restaurant on their coffee break and sit at a table covered with a long tablecloth. One has a newspaper under his arm. After ordering coffee, the one with the newspaper (Man 1) pulls it out and begins to read. He shares some of the news stories briefly with his friend, then whistles in surprise:

Man 1: Did you see this item about the sneak thief?
Man 2: No, what happened?
Man 1: Listen to this. *(Reads aloud)* "Another series of bizarre robberies occurred yesterday in *(name of local town)*. Purses, wallets, and other items mysteriously disappeared. Police are baffled and have no clues as to the thief's identity or how he strikes without being seen. The public is warned to be on their guard until the thief is apprehended."
Man 2: That's unbelievable!

They continue to talk. The waitress brings the coffee, and one man signs the check. They drink the coffee quickly. One man looks at his watch and says, "Hey—we'd better get back to the office." They both rise and walk out—minus their trousers and clad in bright-colored swim trunks. (The two will have to practice getting out of their pants so that the audience doesn't notice. Supposedly, the long tablecloth hides the whole operation, but it still takes some practice to pull it off—no pun intended. A hint—if your actors wear loafers, they'll be able to get their shoes off and on more easily and less noticeably.)

SUMO WRESTLERS

For this skit you'll need two guys, preferably of a muscular or flabby physique, dressed in diapers (use a white sheet for the diapers). You will also need an announcer with a good voice and something he or she can use as a microphone, such as a vacuum hose.

Have the two wrestlers come stomping into the room, circling each other and snorting at each other with deep voices. The announcer introduces the first man as *Yamahaha*, who then steps forward, bows with folded hands and slowly laughs with a deep voice and a Japanese accent, "ha ha ha ha ha." He then throws rice over each shoulder. This procedure is repeated when the announcer introduces *Korimoto-ho*, who responds with a "ho ho ho ho."

After their introductions, the two wrestlers begin fighting. They are never to touch each other or to speak, except for occasional "ha ha's" and "ho ho's." The fight is conducted by each fighter doing to himself what he really wants to do to his opponent. The opponent responds—at the same time—by reacting to the hold or punch as if it had really happened to him.

While this is going on, the announcer calls the play-by-play, describing finger bends, nostril lifts, toe stomps, navel jabs, and armpit hair pulls. With some good actors this event can be hilarious.

THE STAND-IN

Here's a great "pie in the face" skit that involves seven characters. The "sucker" should be played by someone who can play dumb and is a good sport.

Characters:

director (wearing a beret, scarf, and dark glasses)
cameraman (with a "movie camera" of some kind. Try using an old-fashioned meat grinder on a tripod to look like a camera.)
makeup man (with a sack of flour and a powder puff)
the hero (handsome, dressed in white)
the beautiful girl
bartender (or soda jerk)
the sucker (the stand-in)

The skit begins on a movie set. The hero is sitting in a chair next to the girl, getting ready to kiss her, and the cameraman is moving around taking pictures, the director is directing, the lights are on. The "sucker," who is the dumb type, walks into the action, fascinated. He walks in front of the camera.

Sucker: Wow. A real movie. Gosh, I wish I could be in a movie.
Director: *(in a rage)* CUT! CUT! You! Get out of here! You've just ruined a perfect take! Beat it! Scram!
Sucker: *(Slinks off, disappointed.)* Shucks. I shore wish I could be a movie star.
Director: *(Thinks a second.)* Hey, wait a minute! You! *(to the sucker)* Do you want to be in a movie? I think we can use you! *(He whispers something to the hero, and they both smile.)*

Sucker: *(overjoyed)* Really? Wow! I'm a star! Oh, boy! Where do I start? Where are my lines?

Director: Just wait and we'll show you.

The action continues, and the hero sits again by the girl, says a bunch of mushy things to her, and then starts to kiss her. When he does, the girl brings back her hand to slap the hero's face.

Director: Cut! O.K., bring in the stand-in. *(The sucker takes the place of the hero in the chair.)* Makeup! *(The makeup man comes in and throws a bunch of flour in the sucker's face.)* Action!

The sucker starts to kiss the girl, and she slaps him across the face so hard that he falls clean over backwards in his chair.

Director: Cut! Great! All right, let's have scene two . . . action!!!

The hero crawls along the floor, crying "Water, water—give me some water . . ."

Director: Cut! Bring in the stand-in. *(He comes in and takes the hero's place.)* Makeup! *(Makeup man throws more flour in his face.)* Action! Roll-em!

The sucker crawls along the ground and yells "Water!" An offstage helper brings in a big bucket of water and dumps it all over him.

Director: Cut! Perfect! All right, let's have scene three . . . action!

The hero walks up to a bar and orders some milk. The bartender gives him some milk and he drinks it. Then he orders some pie. The bartender says, "Do you *really* want some pie?" The hero says, "Yeah. Gimme some pie." The bartender reaches for the pie.

Director: Cut! Bring in the stand-in! *(The sucker enters, looking pretty bewildered at the whole thing.)* Makeup! *(more flour in the face)* Action!

The sucker stands at the bar, demands the pie, and the bartender throws the pie (big cream pie) in his face.

Director: Cut! Perfect! Tremendous! Well, that's it for today!

Everybody leaves, leaving the stand-in with a puzzled look on his face. He shrugs his shoulders and walks off the stage.

STATUE IN THE PARK

One person poses as a statue behind a park bench or seat.

Two people come along to eat lunch—but the statue, unnoticed by them, takes some of their lunch whenever it is left on the seat. The eaters look more and more suspiciously at each other until they finally leave in disgust.

A couple then approaches and sits down at one end of the seat. They are in the early stages of courtship and sit rather shyly next to each other, with no physical contact. After a while, the statue puts an arm around the girl, who slaps the boy's face and stomps off. Then comes a gardener with a bucket, mop, and feather duster. First he cleans the seat, then looks up at the statue. He dusts the statue with the feather duster, while the person posing tries not to move, sneeze, or laugh. He is about to put the mop into the bucket when there is a voice calling him offstage. He looks at his watch, yells out "I'm coming," picks up the bucket and throws the contents over the statue.

TADPOLES SKIT

For this skit you need two cheap-but-playable guitars you can break up. You need two guys, at least one of whom can play the guitar. (It works best to use the group leaders, such as the youth director or sponsors.) They are introduced to the group as the new folk-singing group, the Tadpoles! The two guys enter with guitars, and here's what happens:

1. Guy #1 (Bob) starts singing off-key, annoying guy #2 (Mike). Mike insults Bob for his singing and with his finger snaps a string on Bob's guitar by pulling it and letting go.
2. Mike starts singing—but Bob stops him, takes out a pair of wirecutters and snips all of Bob's strings except one.
3. Bob starts singing again—but Mike stops him, takes his guitar away, picks up a saw and saws off the neck of Bob's guitar, and hands it back to him.
4. Bob then puts his guitar down and walks over and turns Mike's guitar over, so that the back of the guitar is facing the audience (with Mike still holding it). Bob sticks a target on the back of the guitar, picks up a hammer, and smashes a big hole in it.
5. Mike then takes Bob's guitar, puts it on the floor by a chair, and gets up on the chair, ready to jump on it. He counts One! Two! Three! and jumps—but before he lands, Bob puts Mike's guitar on top of his and Mike smashes both of them.
6. They both pick up their guitars, try to put them together as well as possible, and then finish their song and leave.

This skit, obviously, is pure slapstick—and it requires some tasteful deadpan, Laurel and Hardy-type acting by both guys. The results are hilarious. You can sometimes get damaged or secondhand guitars free or very cheap from some merchants, and don't forget the old junkers you can find at garage sales.

TEENAGE RUMBLE

You'll need about ten guys who dress up like members of a teenage gang, with leather jackets, knives, and chains. The scene is a dark alley, and two gangs meet there for what appears to be a gang war (five of the guys are one gang, five are the other). As the gangs approach each other, they begin shouting and pushing each other around, and finally one of the gang leaders speaks: "You guys going to play our game?" He repeats this several times, and the other gang leader replies, "No way, man, we're not going to play your game!" The first gang leader then pulls out a gun (blank gun) and shoots the second gang leader, who falls and puts on a good dying act. The first gang leader then looks threateningly at the other gang and says, "O.K.—you guys gonna play our game now?" The other gang, sullen and defiant in defeat, says, "Yeah—we'll play your game." Both gangs then lay down all their weapons, get in a circle, join hands, and begin singing, "Ring around the rosie, pocket full of posies, ashes, ashes, we all fall down. . . ."

TUG-O-WAR SKIT

You'll need a room with two doors up front—or a room divider that blocks out the view of the audience. This skit should take place while someone else is talking, so that it distracts the attention of the audience. A boy will come out of one of the doors tugging for all he's worth on a heavy rope. Struggling, he pulls it across the stage and out the other door. A second or two later, while the rope is still moving across the stage, he reappears in the first door on the other end of the same rope, except this time he's pulling vainly against the tugging as he is dragged across the stage and out the second door.

THE TWELVE DAYS OF SCHOOL

Here's a fun song that the group can sing, or you can do it as a skit with one person taking each line and acting out each part. It should be sung to the same tune as the "Twelve Days of Christmas."

"On the first day of school, my mommy said to me . . ."
first day: "Don't ever wet your pants."
second day: "Don't lift your dress."
third day: "Don't eat your crayons."
fourth day: "Don't chew gum."
fifth day: "Don't pick your nose."
sixth day: "Don't hold hands."
seventh day: "Don't throw spitballs."
eighth day: "Don't ever belch."
ninth day: "Don't sleep in class."
tenth day: "Don't be a sissy."
eleventh day: "Don't bite your toenails."
twelfth day: "Don't kiss the girls (boys)."

THE W.C.

Here's a simple one that always gets a laugh. Just give the following background information, then read the letter that follows:

An wealthy English lady, while visiting in Switzerland, was looking for a room and asked the schoolmaster if he could recommend one. He took her to see several rooms, and when everything was settled, the lady returned home to make final preparations to move. When she arrived home, the thought occurred to her that she had not seen a "W. C." in the place. (In England, a W. C. is a "water closet" or a bathroom.)

So she immediately wrote a note to the schoolmaster asking him if there was a W. C. in the place. But the schoolmaster, who spoke very poor English, had never heard of a W. C. and asked the parish priest for help. Together they tried to find the meaning of the letters—and the only solution they could find was "Wayside Chapel." The schoolmaster then wrote the following letter to the English lady:

My Dear Madam:

I take great pleasure in informing you that the W.C. is situated nine miles from the house in the center of a beautiful grove of pine trees surrounded by lovely grounds.

It is capable of holding 229 people, and it is open on Sundays and Thursdays only. As there are a great number of people expected during the summer months, I suggest that you come early, although usually there is plenty of standing room. This is an unfortunate situation, especially if you are in the habit of going regularly. It may be of some interest to know that my daughter was married in the W.C. and it was there that she met her husband. I can remember the rush there was for seats. There were ten people to every seat usually occupied by one. It was wonderful to see the expressions on their faces.

You will be glad to hear that a good number of people bring their lunch and make a day of it, while those who can afford to go by car, arrive just on time. I would especially recommend your ladyship to go on Thursdays when there is an organ accompaniment. The acoustics are excellent, and even the most delicate sounds can be heard everywhere.

The newest addition is a bell donated by a wealthy resident of the district. It rings every time a person enters. A bazaar is to be held to provide for plush seats for all, since the people feel it is long needed. My wife is rather delicate so she cannot attend regularly. It is almost a year since she went last, and naturally it pains her very much not to be able to go more often.

I shall be delighted to reserve the best seat for you, where you shall be seen by all. For the children, there is a special day and time so that they do not disturb the elders. Hoping to be of some service to you,

The Schoolmaster

CHAPTER THREE

FAMOUS
INTERVIEWS

THE BERMUDA TRIANGLE

This interview is between Luther Capehart, a talk show host, and Horace Q. Quivermayer, the "Bermuda Triangle Man." Use a typical talk show set—two chairs, a coffee table, and maybe a plastic plant.

Luther:	Hello and welcome to "Put Up or Shut Up," a talk show where, each week, we try to find something new and interesting to talk about. Of course sometimes that isn't as easy as it sounds, but this week I'm sure we've got a winner. Well, I'm not sure, but I *hope* we have a winner. My name is Luther Capehart and tonight our guest is Mr. Horace Q. Quivermayer. Mr. Quivermayer will be discussing with us the mysterious and interesting, we hope, secret of the Bermuda Triangle. Welcome, Mr. Quivermayer.
Quivermayer:	Thank you.
Luther:	My notes tell me that you are one of the kissing. Just what does that mean?
Quivermayer:	I have no idea.
Luther:	You have no idea?
Quivermayer:	Not an inkling.
Luther:	(*uneasily looking offstage for an explanation*) What? Oh. (*back to Quivermayer*) My aides tell me the notes should read "one of the missing." (*corrects with pen*) Must be a typographical error. Are you indeed one of the missing?
Quivermayer:	That I am.
Luther:	Aha. Now we're getting somewhere. Where are you missing from?
Quivermayer:	At the moment everywhere. I am originally missing from Willow Wisp, Missouri.
Luther:	And how did you come to be missing?
Quivermayer:	Do you mean, how did I happen to fall into the mysterious secret of the Bermuda Triangle?
Luther:	Exactly.
Quivermayer:	Well, it all started on our homemade sloop, The Abalone. I was with my wife, my three kids, and Bunky, our dog. We were sailing along—
Luther:	You were sailing along—

Quivermayer:	On Moonlight Bay—
Luther:	On Moonlight Bay—
Quivermayer:	We could hear the voices singing—
Luther:	What did they seem to say?
Quivermayer:	I haven't the foggiest. That was the moment we fell into the mysterious secret of the Bermuda Triangle.
Luther:	That's when you disappeared.
Quivermayer:	That was the moment.
Luther:	What was it like?
Quivermayer:	Pardon me?
Luther:	What was it like? Tell us what happened after you fell into the mysterious secret of the Bermuda Triangle.
Quivermayer:	Oh, I couldn't do that.
Luther:	Pardon me?
Quivermayer:	I couldn't tell you about what happened.
Luther:	Why not?
Quivermayer:	It wouldn't be a mysterious secret then, would it?
Luther:	I see. Well, could you tell us about the accommodations without giving away the location?
Quivermayer:	I don't think so.
Luther:	Just a hint?
Quivermayer:	Nope.
Luther:	How about a mailing address in case some of the folks want to get in touch with you?
Quivermayer:	I'm afraid not.
Luther:	A box number?
Quivermayer:	No.
Luther:	In that case, since we seem to have covered as much as we can, Mr. Quivermayer, I'd like to thank you for not being here tonight.
Quivermayer:	My pleasure.

THE BOXER

This interview is between a television sportscaster, dressed in a topcoat and holding a microphone, and the boxer, wearing boxer shorts, boxing gloves, and a robe. As the skit begins, the boxer enters shadowboxing, dancing around, and yelling "I am the greatest!" and other exclamations.

Sportscaster:	Ladies and Gentlemen, tonight on ABC's Wild World of Sports, we take you into the ring here at Madison Square Garden for an on-the-spot chat with lower-Eastside's pride and joy, Rocky "Kid" Canvasback. Rocky, how do you like being on nationwide TV?
Rocky:	Hiya, Mom! Hiya, Dad! *(Laughs.)*
Sportscaster:	What's so funny?
Rocky:	I'm an orphan.

Sportscaster:	I understand you have an outdoor bout in Montreal next February. Won't it be kind of cold?
Rocky:	No, we wear gloves.
Sportscaster:	By the way, Rocky, how old are you?
Rocky:	Thirty-eight years old.
Sportscaster:	How did you get started in the fight business?
Rocky:	When I was a kid I was real tough. I could lick any kid on the block, except the Jones's.
Sportscaster:	Why couldn't you beat the Jones kids?
Rocky:	They were boys.
Sportscaster:	How many fights have you had?
Rocky:	101. Won them all except the first 100. Got a winning streak going now.
Sportscaster:	Why did you quit the fight business?
Rocky:	Broke my hand.
Sportscaster:	Hitting an opponent I suppose?
Rocky:	No, the referee stepped on it.
Sportscaster:	By the way, how old did you say you were?
Rocky:	Fifty-two.
Sportscaster:	Fought a lot of people in your time, all kinds and sizes. What do you think of big men?
Rocky:	Big men, eh? Well, I think the bigger they are the harder they hit.
Sportscaster:	Tell us, Rocky, did you ever fight any of the world champs?
Rocky:	Yeah, Joe Louis in the Olympic Arena. Had him really scared in the first round.
Sportscaster:	Was it your powerful right that scared him?
Rocky:	No—he thought he had killed me.
Sportscaster:	When you get knocked out like that, I suppose they carry you out on a stretcher, don't they?
Rocky:	No, I wear handles on my trunks.
Sportscaster:	How old did you say you were?
Rocky:	Sixty-eight.
Sportscaster:	Lot in the news about fixing fights, lately. Anybody ever ask you to throw one?

Rocky:	Yeah, I remember I was fighting Tiger Mills in Dallas, Texas. They asked me to take a dive in the sixth round.
Sportscaster:	But you didn't do it, did you?
Rocky:	Nope—I never got to the sixth round.
Sportscaster:	Anything unusual ever happen?
Rocky:	Yeah, I remember the time I was fighting Honey Boy, Dave Lawrence in New York City. He smashed me right in the nose in the first round, but it didn't bleed until the fifth.
Sportscaster:	How come?
Rocky:	Tired blood.
Sportscaster:	I understand most boxers wear a mouth piece. Ever give you any trouble?
Rocky:	No, not usually, only when I'm eating.
Sportscaster:	How old are you?
Rocky:	Seventy-nine. What's the matter, you punchy or something?
Sportscaster:	Tell me, Rocky—I've got a young kid, fourteen years old, who wants to get into boxing. Have you got any advice for him?
Rocky:	You got a kid? Yeah . . . my advice, eat well, live clean, keep breathing, in and out, in and out, stop for more than three minutes you're a real goner. Then go around hitting people.
Sportscaster:	Any people?
Rocky:	No, just little people—you see a kid, hit him. You see a dog, kick it, good for the footwork. Live clean, hit hard, and keep breathing.
Sportscaster:	Give Rocky an exit.

CHRISTOPHER COLUMBUS

This interview takes place on the "Santa Maria," a ship on its way to discover America. The reporter should wear a topcoat and carry a hand-held microphone, and "Columbus" can look like any typical Portuguese sea captain.

Reporter:	*(holding microphone)* This is Cameron-Cameron Holmes, coming to you from the ship Santa Maria, far out in the unknown sea. The year is 1483. We're waiting to see if we can get an interview with the famed Christopher Columbus.

Columbus: *(talking to the men of his ship)* Come on, men, let's get this ship moving faster. Pull up another sail! Quit that sleeping on deck and get to your duties. We've got to discover the new world. I know you're cold and hungry. This voyage is a hardship for all of us. But think of the adventure of it, and the great service you'll be doing to mankind by proving the world is round. You are all great sailors, men, and you and our ship will never be forgotten because we set forth with courage and faith to discover the new world.

Reporter: Excuse me, Admiral Columbus. Could I have a word with you?

Columbus: *(still talking to men)* Yes, men—think of it! The first to see the new world! No longer will you be prisoners in the dungeons of Spain, but notable men of the sea!

Reporter: Excuse me, Admiral Columbus. May I ask you a few questions?

Columbus: Oh, pardon me, young man. I didn't know you were here.

Reporter: Columbus, that was certainly an inspiring challenge to your sailors. How long have you been out to sea?

Columbus: Fifteen minutes.

Reporter: I see. Columbus, how do you handle being away from home, out on the ocean, for such a long period of time? After all, it's a long way to the new world.

Columbus: Well, it's because I love the sea. And I love this ship. I'm married to this ship, mister, and that's the finest wife a man could ever have!

Reporter: That's very romantic. Oh, by the way, what are those other two ships following along behind?

Columbus: Those are the kids. We call them Pinta and Niña. Cute little rascals, aren't they? They take after their mother.

Reporter: Columbus, what compels a man of your character to set sail for the purpose of discovering the new world?

Columbus: It's because I love poetry. I write poetry, you see. I don't really care what I discover. I just want a poem.

Reporter: What kind of a poem do you want?

Columbus: Oh, just a simple little poem about me. You know . . . one all the school kids could learn and remember my name by. I've been doing some writing. Listen to this. "In fourteen hundred and eighty-three, Columbus sailed as fast as a bee." I know it's not real good, but it's a start. What do you think?

Reporter: Well . . . what about this? "In fourteen hundred and eighty-three, beneath the swaying chestnut tree."

Columbus: Yeah, that's the idea. I like that very much. But you *left out my name*. Here's another. "In fourteen hundred and eighty-three, Columbus exhibited his gallantry." That's still not it, but it's got to ring something like that.

Reporter: Yeah, I see what you mean. What about this one: "In fourteen hundred and eighty-three, upon the ship, upon the sea, in the midst of the storm—always courageous was our sailor, never forlorn."

Columbus: That's it! That's great! *(pause)* But you *left my name out again!* Here's another one. It has all the essentials. "In fourteen hundred and eighty-three, Columbus is the boy for me." It's still not exactly what I want, but that's the idea.

Reporter: How about this: "In fourteen hundred and ninety-two, Columbus sailed the ocean blue."

Columbus: That's it! That's it! That's *exactly* what I've been looking for!

Reporter: But, Columbus—1492 is nine years from now.

Columbus: Who cares! All I want is a poem. *(to men on ship)* O.K., men, we're turning back. Turn this ship back toward Spain. We'll come back in *nine years!*

THE CROPDUSTER

This interview takes place between the Master of Ceremonies and his special guest, Dusty Crashalot, the world famous cropduster. Dusty should look as ridiculous as possible. You'll need an old World War I pilot's hat and goggles, combat boots, and other props that the script calls for.

M.C.:   Today it is our privilege to have with us one of the men who has made America great. Risking life and limb daily, he pursues his dangerous task with the calm, cool nerve of a man who is truly one of the great adventurers of modern times. His is the skill that has contributed so much to the wealth and beauty of our country and the abundance of our harvest. A real warm hand for one of California's foremost cropdusters . . . Dusty Crashalot! *(Enter Dusty, throwing flour from a paper bag.)*

M.C.:   Well, it's really great to have you with us today, Dusty. Just how long have you been a cropduster?

Dusty: Well, let's see now . . . mmm . . . ah . . . two weeks. Yeah, that's right. Two weeks!

M.C.: Two weeks? That's not a very long time.

Dusty: Well, a cropduster's life expectancy isn't very long either. We can only get one kind of insurance, you know.

M.C.: You can get insurance? I thought your job was so dangerous that you couldn't get insurance at all.

Dusty: Yes, I can. I'm fully covered for childbirth.

M.C.: I see. Dusty, were you ever a commercial pilot before you became a cropduster?

Dusty: Oh, yes. I was a pilot on a cattle ranch.

M.C.: A cattle ranch? What does a pilot on a cattle ranch do?

Dusty: *(Acts like he's shoveling.)* Oh, I just pilot here, pilot there, just piling it wherever I can pilot.

M.C.: Well, I meant, didn't you ever fly an airplane?

Dusty: *(Pulls paper airplane from pocket.)* Oh, yes, why I flew one all the way from the back of the room to the blackboard once.

M.C.: No, I mean while you dust crops. Don't you fly an airplane while you dust crops?

Dusty: Oh, no—that would be too dangerous. You have to have your hands free to dip in the sack!

M.C.: I see . . . but . . .

Dusty: Well, I guess you could fly the plane with your feet, but you sure can't dip in the sack with your feet!

M.C.: What kind of equipment do you use in your work, Dusty?

Dusty: Well, usually a whisk broom, or a feather duster. I just walk up and down the rows dusting off the plants. They have to breathe, you know.

M.C.: You actually dust the crops with a feather duster?

Dusty: Well, once I used one of my wife's wigs, but she really blew her top!

M.C.: What is the main crop that you dust, Dusty?

Dusty: Well, let's see . . . that would be the potunge!

M.C.: What is a potunge?

Dusty: Well, it's a cross between a potato and a sponge.

M.C.: Sounds interesting. Does it taste good?

Dusty: No, it tastes terrible, but, man, it sure soaks up the gravy!

M.C.: Dusty, do you ever work in cotton?

Dusty: No, most of my underclothes are Japanese silk!

M.C.:   Dusty, tell us about your most exciting experience as a cropduster.

Dusty: Well, that would be when I flew so high in my plane, that the field below looked like a postage stamp. I sent my plane into a power dive and crashed to earth!

M.C.:   Did you hit the field?

Dusty: What field? It *was* a postage stamp!

M.C.:   Have you ever had any other experiences like that, Dusty?

Dusty: Well, one time my plane lost all power at 10,000 feet!

M.C.:   Really? That's bad!

Dusty: Not too bad. I had my chute on.

M.C.:   That's good.

Dusty: Not too good. It wouldn't open.

M.C.:   Oooooh . . . that's bad!

Dusty: Not too bad. I was headed straight for a haystack.

M.C.:   Well, that's good.

Dusty: No, that was bad! There was a pitchfork in the haystack.

M.C.:   Oh, that is bad.

Dusty: Not too bad . . . I missed the pitchfork.

M.C.:   That's good.

Dusty: No, that's bad. I missed the haystack too!!

THE FIRECHIEF

For this skit, you need three people: the announcer, the reporter ("Walter Crankcase"), and "Mr. Firechief."

Announcer: The scene is the great San Francisco fire of 1906. This horrible devastating inferno is now in its third day of devouring the picturesque city of San Francisco. Millions upon millions of dollars have gone up in smoke. Hundreds have lost their lives, as well as thousands left homeless. This could possibly be called the greatest and most destructive fire to ever occur in the history of the world. We take you back now to this monster of nature for a close-up look at

	what actually happened. Here to bring you an on-the-spot report of this great fire is our roving reporter ... Walter Crankcase.
Crankcase:	This is Walter Crankcase, and we're here in the middle of the great San Francisco fire on the corner of 182nd Street and Kookamunga Avenue, site of the enormous 68-story Biltmore Hotel, which is rapidly being leveled by this ravaging inferno, which has already left thousands homeless and hundreds dead. The most experienced firemen in the world are battling this blaze at this very moment, and we're going to interview the man who is in control of these thousands of firefighters who are trying to salvage the huge Biltmore. He is the most famous firechief of all time. So famous, in fact, that he is known to millions all over the world as "Mr. Firechief." His name: Clarence Firechief. He is presently trying to control the huge blaze, and we're going to step over and have a few words with him.
Firechief:	(shouting) All right, you men! Bring on the trucks! Grab those hoses! Concentrate on the center of the blaze! Keep fighting, men!
Crankcase:	Excuse me, sir.
Firechief:	Yes?
Crankcase:	I'm a roving reporter and we'd like to ask you a few questions. Just how are things going so far?
Firechief:	Not bad. The fire's going pretty good, the people are nice and panicky, and the water supply is about gone, and ...
Crankcase:	Excuse me, but there's a lady getting ready to jump from the 46-story window!
Firechief:	Oh, no! (shouts) You men! Drop those hoses and get the net! A lady's jumpin' over there! Get the net! Get the ... Forget it, men, back to the hoses.
Crankcase:	Gee, Mr. Firechief—that woman just fell to her death!
Firechief:	Very observant.
Crankcase:	Thank you. Now, let's get a little of your background. Just how long have you been a fireman?
Firechief:	All my life. I've had fire on my heart ever since I was a lad of three years.
Crankcase:	Gee, that's amazing.
Firechief:	It is if you like heartburn.
Crankcase:	Why did you become a firechief, Mr. Firechief?
Firechief:	You may not believe this, but I couldn't do anything else.

Crankcase: Why not? You went to school, didn't you?

Firechief: Yeah, but there's no money in throwing spitwads at the teacher!

Crankcase: Did you go to college?

Firechief: Yes, I went to the American Firechief's College. Of all the men who enter American Firechief's College, 90% go on to bigger and better things!

Crankcase: Gee, that's wonderful. But what about the other 10%?

Firechief: They become firechiefs.

Crankcase: I see. Mr. Firechief, can you tell us the difference between a four-alarm fire and a five-alarm fire?

Firechief: Yes, that's easy. One alarm.

Crankcase: Mr. Firechief, is it true that your fire department has won many awards?

Firechief: Yes, it is. We set a record in answering the alarm. The alarm went off, we got dressed, slid down the pole, got into the trucks, and left the firehouse in two minutes and thirty seconds.

Crankcase: Wow! That's great! What was on fire?

Firechief: The firehouse.

Crankcase: Mr. Firechief, when the alarm goes off, how do you locate the fire?

Firechief: We look under the smoke. There it is.

Crankcase: Mr. Firechief, I understand your father was a hero during the Chicago fire.

Firechief:	That's right. Even during the worst of the blaze, he kept a level head.
Crankcase:	Gee, that's fantastic! What was his secret?
Firechief:	Well, he was in New York City at the time.
Crankcase:	Mr. Firechief, just how many men are on duty right now?
Firechief:	I'm not sure.
Crankcase:	How long has the fire been ablaze?
Firechief:	I don't know.
Crankcase:	Mr. Firechief, do you think that you will ever be fired?
Firechief:	No, that's ridiculous.
Crankcase:	Why is that?
Firechief:	I know too much!
Crankcase:	Mr. Firechief, there may be some kids here tonight who are considering going into the field of firefighting. Do you have anything you'd like to say to them?
Firechief:	Yes, I do. *(Takes mike.)* Attention Future Firemen of America! The job of a fireman is not an easy one. It's a rough road . . . but the rewards are great! You, too, can see thousands left homeless and hundreds dead. But make sure that you want to go through with it. Take the W.E.I.R.D.O. test to find out exactly what job you are best suited for. Thank you.
Crankcase:	And thank you, Mr. Firechief. By the way, did you take the W.E.I.R.D.O. test?
Firechief:	Yes, I did.
Crankcase:	What job did you discover you were best suited for?
Firechief:	Throwing spitwads at teachers. Now if you'll excuse me, I'd like to get back to the fire. I've also got a hobby I'd kinda like to get back to.
Crankcase:	A hobby?
Firechief:	That's right. I'm a firebug. *(Shouts.)* All right, you men! Let's get this thing put out! Don't give up! *(Exit.)*

HERKIMER, THE ALL AMERICAN

For this skit, you need the "Coach" (who does the interview) and "Herkimer," the football player. All the coach needs is a whistle and a hat, and Herkimer should be dressed as ridiculously as possible, in old football gear.

Coach: Hi, everyone! It's good to be here to tell you a little about the inside of football—what players think and how plays are really born. All of the really hard work of making a good football team. At this time I would like to introduce one of our real star players to help inform you! *(Yells offstage.)* HERKIMER! *(Enter big player with little boy's uniform and helmet on backwards—also girl's purse tucked in pants so audience can't see it.)*

Coach: Aw, come on, Herk, you got your helmet on backwards.

Herk: Well, you told me I was gonna be a catcher and I don't want to get hit in the nose!

Coach: I didn't say catcher. I said an end who catches passes. Look, Herk, I think I made a mistake putting you at end.

Herk: Whaddaya mean mistake? Last game I had three completions in a row.

Coach: Yeah, I know, Herk—but we call them interceptions when the other team gets the ball!

Herk: Gee, Coach, you said don't let the ball touch the ground and that big guy said he had it so I thought I'd "let him have it."

Coach: Well, Herk, I'm gonna change your position anyway—you're just not rough enough!

Herk: Not rough enough! Last game I got in a fight right on the field.

Coach: You did? What happened—did somebody hit you?

Herk:	Yeah—this big guy. *(Pulls out purse.)* So I just took my purse and hit him. *(Starts beating coach.)*
Coach:	O.K., O.K., Herk, but I'm gonna change you to a half-back anyway!
Herk:	Oh, please, Coach, not that—I need all my back. It's not very big anyway!
Coach:	No, Herk, it's a position on the field. Here, let me show you a play. *(Has a play diagrammed on board—x's and o's.)* You see, Herk, you take the ball from the quarterback. This man blocks here, this one there, and this one here, then you run for a touchdown!
Herk:	Really—ME?
Coach:	Sure—you! Do you have any questions?
Herk:	Just one—what are all those x's and o's?
Coach:	Forget it! Here, let me give you our schedule so you can really get jazzed up! *(Herk starts pawing ground and snorting.)* Next week we play the Brownies!
Herk:	The Brownies—WOW!
Coach:	The next week the Girl Scouts. *(Herk roars and claws the air.)* After that the Bluebirds.
Herk:	Bluebirds! The varsity!
Coach:	And our last game is the Los Angeles Rams!
Herk:	Nyaaa!
Coach:	Does anyone on that list scare you?
Herk:	Just one . . . the Bluebirds!
Coach:	Yeah—they do have pretty tough girls! Well, Herk, we're running out of time. Is there anything you would like to pass on to the young boys that would help them?
Herk:	Uh, yeah—just take that old football and tuck in under you arm. *(Puts nose near underarm and indicates terrible odor.)* On second thought, better not do that—it'll rot! Carry it out here *(Grips it with fingertips, arms outstretched.)* and just GO GO GO! *(Runs out.)*

THE INCREDIBLE KIDNAPPING

This interview is between Luther Capehart, the talk show host, and Ronald Albert Forkman, the man with an incredible story to tell. The set is a typical television talk show, with chairs, table, plants, and the like. You will also need a book, a record album, some tapes, a lighter, and an ashtray.

Luther: Good evening and welcome to *Put Up or Shut Up*, the talk show where we probe and examine the strange and the unusual. Tonight our guest certainly is strange and unusual—I mean, his topic is strange and unusual. Our guest tonight is a gentleman who claims to have been kidnapped by aliens and taken to the Bermuda Triangle. Please welcome, all the way from Cape May, New Jersey, Mr. Ronald Albert Forkman. Hello, Mr. Forkman.

Forkman: Hello.

Luther: You claim, Mr. Forkman, to have been kidnapped by aliens and taken to the Bermuda Triangle.

Forkman: Yes, that's right. It all began in my backyard. I was digging my begonias in the garden. I always like to do that when no one else is home because the wife intensely dislikes begonias and the kids are always playing in the dirt. You know how kids are.

Luther: Yes.

Forkman: Well, anyway, they—the aliens—snuck up behind me and slapped something over my head.

Luther: *(to audience)* Some sort of complex computer-like brain-numbing device, no doubt.

Forkman: Actually, it was a paper sack.

Luther: I beg your pardon?

Forkman: A paper sack, like the kind you get from a grocery store.

Luther: I see.

Forkman: Then one of the aliens shouted, "Don't make any trouble and you won't get hurt. We're from the Bermuda Triangle."

Luther: Uh-huh. What happened next?

Forkman: They sort of pushed me into the kitchen and started asking me questions.

Luther: What did they want to know?

Forkman: Oh, they asked questions like, "Where does your wife keep her jewelry?" "How much cash have you got on you?" "Where's your wallet?" "Is the color TV in your bedroom?"

Luther: Ahh, Mr. Forkman . . .

Forkman: They told me I had been chosen the most likely human and that was why they were borrowing all my possessions. They wanted to study them, they said, so they could promote a better understanding between our two races.

Luther: Mr. Forkman . . .

Forkman: Wait, there's more. After about half an hour they put me in the back of their truck and—

Luther: They were driving a truck?

Forkman: I questioned that, too. But they explained to me that you can't land a giant space ship in the middle of Cape May, New Jersey, without attracting a certain amount of attention. They didn't want to do that, you see.

Luther: Mr. Forkman . . .

Forkman: Then they took me to their hideout, er, headquarters, where we waited to be picked up by a shuttle craft.

Luther: And the shuttle craft took you to their underwater city?

Forkman: It was fantastic! The city is all enclosed in a big glass bubble. They've got huge skyscrapers that they call "sky bumpers" because they don't really scrape the sky, they just sort of bump it. Because everything is round, you see.

Luther: Uh-huh.

Forkman: And all the people drive around in things called "air bubbles." The passengers are suspended on a hammock in the center of the bubble. This keeps them upright as the bubbles roll. They have half-ton truck bubbles. School bus bubbles. Yellow cab bubbles.

Luther: You saw these bubble vehicles?

Forkman: Sure!

Luther: Really?

Forkman: Well—no. Not really. I had to keep the sack on my head. But I asked the guys I was with and they filled me in.

Luther: In other words, you have no firsthand observation of this "underwater city." Only what "the guys" told you.

Forkman: Well, yeah.

Luther: When they released you, what did they tell you?

Forkman:	To count to three thousand and that I shouldn't try to contact the Air Force, the Coast Guard, the F.A.A., or the police.
Luther:	And where were you when you finally took the sack off?
Forkman:	Yeah, well, they said they had to allow for wind drift . . .
Luther:	Where were you?
Forkman:	In my neighbor's swimming pool.
Luther:	Did they ever return any of the items they took?
Forkman:	Not exactly.
Luther:	*(after a short pause)* I'm afraid you'll have to leave now, Mr. Forkman.
Forkman:	What do you mean?
Luther:	I mean, Mr. Forkman, that you have obviously been the victim of a routine, if a tad imaginative, burglary and now you are trying to recoup some of your losses by turning yourself into a public spectacle. I, for one, refuse to be a party to it.
Forkman:	I don't know what you're talking about. *(Decides to get his plugs in while he can.)* Do you mean, just because I've written a book about my adventures *(produces previously hidden book)* called, *Where I've Been and What They Say I've Stood Next To*, and because I've got an album *(produces album)* coming out, also available in 8-track and cassette *(produces tapes)*, because of this you doubt my word? . . .
Luther:	That's just about enough, Mr. Forkman. *(to audience)* I apologize, ladies and gentlemen. Until next time, thank you and goodnight. *(Exits.)*
Forkman:	*(yelling after Luther)* I'll prove I was there! Look! They gave me souvenirs! Look! They gave me this lighter and ashtray set! *(Produces lighter and ashtray.)* Look! "Hello from the Bermuda Triangle!" *(Stands and follows Luther.)* What about that, huh?

THE LONE RANGER

This is an interview between Abner Theobald Knucklenose the third and an aging Lone Ranger. The Lone Ranger can be dressed like the famous cowboy hero, but as ridiculously as possible. Knucklenose should be wearing a large safari hat, thick glasses, and a big false nose.

A.T.K.:   Good evening, ladies and gentlemen, I'm your Famous Interviews Interviewer, Abner Theobald Knucklenose III, presenting another in an ongoing series of (Ta-da!) "Famous Interviews." This evening "Famous Interviews" will be interviewing a person whom you all will indeed recognize and look up to—that world-renowned masked man of the West—that man who dared to stand alone against thieves and hombres—that elusive agent of the Texas Rangers—comrade to his faithful Indian companion "Tonto." Yes, ladies and gentlemen, may I introduce to you . . . in person . . . the one and only . . . the Lone Ranger!

Lone: Hi-yo-Silver, away! *(Lone Ranger—obviously greatly overweight—comes out galloping on a stick-horse. He prances around for a few seconds trying to tame Silver down.)* Whoa, boy! Easy, big fella! *(Finally Silver settles down. Lone Ranger dismounts.)* Lie down, boy. *(Lone Ranger drops stick-horse.)*

A.T.K.:   It certainly is a delight to have you with us this evening, Mr. Ranger.

Lone: Why, thank ya, young "whippersnapper." But just call me "Lone."

A.T.K.:   Well, Mr. Ranger, I personally am thrilled that you are with us. I'm a big fan of yours.

Lone: Thanks, but just call me "Lone," if ya don't mind, son.

A.T.K.:   Yes, but—you see, I have such a high respect for you, I could never call you by your first name, Mr. Ranger.

Lone: "Lone" is my second name—"The" is my first. But I want ya to call me "Lone," understand? *(He pulls out a six-shooter.)*

A.T.K.:   O.K., O.K. But why do you want me to call you "Lone"?

Lone: You really want to know?

A.T.K.:   Yes, I certainly do, Mr. Ranger—I mean, "Lone."

Lone: I want ya to call me "Lone" 'cause I'm lonely. It's been lonely in the saddle since my horse died. That's why I'm a-ridin' that stick.

A.T.K.:   That's too bad.

Lone: Oh, not that bad. Ol' stick there don't eat no oats. Cheap transportation.

A.T.K.:   Oh, well that's good.

Lone: No, not too good. Seems I'm always gettin' slivers in my britches.

A.T.K.:   I understand that employment for you has been rather difficult since the Wild West was tamed.

Lone:	That's right. I've tried different jobs, but none seem to work out very good. One time I took a job as a professional parachute jumper.
A.T.K.:	Well, that's a real down-to-earth type job. (Laughs.) Get it? "Down-to-earth!" (Laughs again.) Excuse me. How did you like that job?
Lone:	Well, things just didn't open up for me. So I quit. Then I tried selling door-to-door, but that was just a lot of hard knocks.
A.T.K.:	Yes, and sometimes you could get into a jam—door jam, that is.
Lone:	That's right. So then I got an easy job in a clock factory. All I'd do is stand around and make faces. Yeah, times have been rough. Finally, I got a job as a railroad conductor.
A.T.K.:	Oh, is that so?
Lone:	Yeah, but only part-time. I'm a semiconductor.
A.T.K.:	What ever happened to "Tonto"?
Lone:	You mean my *faithful* Indian companion?
A.T.K.:	Yes.
Lone:	Well, one day we were ridin' the range, and a band of Indians started chasin' us. Just as we began to outrun 'em, we noticed another band of Indians comin' at us. We looked to the left—more Indians; to the right—more Indians. We were surrounded. We were doomed. I turned to Tonto and said, "Well, Faithful Indian Companion, this is it. We're done for. We're gonna die."
A.T.K.:	What did he say?
Lone:	He said, "What you mean *we*, paleface?"
A.T.K.:	Well, it certainly seems as though you are the *Lone* Ranger, what with no horse, no job, and no faithful Indian companion. It's kind of sad, isn't it, ladies and gentlemen? Here we have a famous hero of yesteryear—a mere shell of his former glory days. Overweight—run down—without employment—unneeded—kind of looks ridiculous in that mask, doesn't he? (Laughs.)
Lone:	Say, what kind of a name is "Knucklenose," anyway?
A.T.K.:	Well, ladies and gentlemen, that's all the time we have tonight. Join us again soon for another (Ta-da!) "Famous Interview."

THE PROFESSOR AND THE STARS

The interviewer can be a talk-show host or a news reporter. Professor Blanktop, a very unusual astronomer, can be dressed as an eccentric scientist and speak with a foreign dialect. Be creative.

Interviewer: *(Holds paper and pencil.)* Good evening, Professor Blanktop. We feel very fortunate to be able to interview one of the world's greatest astronomers. For our first question, professor, do you think the moon is really inhabited?

Professor: *(oddly dressed and speaks just as oddly)* Inhabited? What's this word "inhabited"?

Interviewer: I mean . . . do you think people live there?

Professor: Why didn't you say so? Of course people live on the moon. *(gesture)* I talk with them every night.

Interviewer: *(amazed)* You talk with moon-people every night? Through thousands of miles of space? But how is that possible?

Professor: *(Shrugs.)* We talk in loud voices.

Interviewer:	(Sighs.) Professor, tell us—what is the most interesting thing you have ever seen through your telescope?
Professor:	(Frowns in puzzlement.) My what-a-scope?
Interviewer:	(impatiently) Your telescope! Telescope!
Professor:	(brightly) Oh, yes, that long thing. (Pretends to hold telescope to eye.) Well, the most interesting thing I've seen is the new comet named Susanna Smith.
Interviewer:	You've seen a new comet which you've named after an old girl friend?
Professor:	No, I've seen a new girl friend whom I've named after an old comet named Susanna Smith.
Interviewer:	But how come you saw a girl when you were looking up like this? (Pretends to hold telescope to eye, pointed toward sky.)
Professor:	Because when I was looking up like this (Pretends to look through telescope toward sky.) I found it more interesting to look down like this. (Lowers telescope so that he's looking slightly down, as if at the street.)
Interviewer:	But why do you call your lady friend a comet?
Professor:	(Sadly shrugs.) Every time I ask her for a date (zoom palm through air) she zooms away.
Interviewer:	(Shake head.) I see. Now then, I understand that you believe that a man on Mars has three ears. Isn't that rather strange?
Professor:	(Shrugs.) What's so strange? He has three eyes.
Interviewer:	Professor Blanktop, it is a proven fact that the earth circles the sun, yet I recently heard you say that the sun circles the earth.
Professor:	That is right. What is your question?
Interviewer:	But how can you say the sun circles the earth?
Professor:	Very simple. I say it like this: (Holds up finger, speaks in monotone.) The-sun-circles-the-earth. (Shrugs.) Very easy to say.
Interviewer:	I see. Tell us, professor, in what direction is the planet Jupiter?
Professor:	(Points upward.) Up.
Interviewer:	(Shrugs.) Most astronomers work at night, but I understand you prefer day work. Why is that?
Professor:	Less stars, less work.
Interviewer:	Professor Blanktop, what first got you interested in astronomy?
Professor:	My mother. She told me to hitch my wagon to a star.

Interviewer:	By that she meant you should be ambitious, that you should strive for great things.
Professor:	*(sourly)* Is *that* what she meant?
Interviewer:	Tell us, professor, what is there about the moon that's so romantic? I mean, why do lovers always sit under the moon?
Professor:	*(with authority)* Lovers have to sit under the moon. *(gesture left)* Sit over there—you're under the moon. *(gesture to right)* Sit over there—you're under the moon. No matter where you sit you're under the moon; even haters sit under the moon.
Interviewer:	*(Nods.)* Very logical, professor. Tell us, how long would it take a rocket ship to reach the planet Mercury?
Professor:	*(Pulls out a large sheet of paper and a pencil, briefly pretends to figure it out, frowns as he crosses out, scribbles, smiles broadly as he finishes.)* Exactly six years, ten days, five hours, eight minutes, and four seconds.
Interviewer:	*(in admiration)* How did you figure it out so fast?
Professor:	*(Shrugs.)* I didn't—it was just a guess.
Interviewer:	*(baffled)* But what were you doing with that pencil and paper?
Professor:	*(Grins, holds up the sheet of paper to reveal a large drawing of a girl, with the name "Susanna" printed below.)* I was sketching Susanna Smith! Pretty?
Interviewer:	*(wearily)* Professor, can't you talk about anything but Susanna Smith?
Professor:	*(Brightly nods.)* Yes! Let's talk about Sylvia Smith.
Interviewer:	Who is Sylvia Smith?
Professor:	*(Turns sheet over to reveal another large picture of a girl with "Sylvia" printed below.)* Susanna's sister. She's even prettier.
Interviewer:	*(Takes a deep breath, shakes head.)* Professor Blanktop, as a final question— do you have any advice to give all those beautiful young people out there who might wish to become astronomers?
Professor:	*(Holds up finger.)* I have just one thing to tell them.
Interviewer:	And that is?
Professor:	*(sternly)* Don't go peeking around for Susanna Smith! *(Walks away, wagging finger at audience.)* Find your own comets! *(Exits.)*

THE ROLLER SKATER

Here's another interview between our affable talk-show host, Luther Capehart, and his special guest Josiah P. Forbes, the roller skater.

Luther: Hello and welcome to Put Up or Shut Up, a talk show where we interview all the top-name performers and newsmakers. *(Remembering who his guest is, he apologizes to the audience.)* And, sometimes, when they're not available we talk to you, the ordinary citizen. My name is Luther Capehart and tonight we have with us a very ordinary citizen, Mr. Josiah P. Forbes. Mr. Forbes is, at this very moment, in the process of setting the world record for wearing a pair of roller skates.

Forbes: *(eager)* I sure am!

Luther: Welcome, Mr. Forbes.

Forbes: Thank you. It's nice to be here.

Luther: It's nice having you here.

Forbes:	Well, it's nice being here.
Luther:	*(trying to get down to business)* I think, Mr. Forbes, we should, at the very outset of the show, point out that you are wearing your roller skates not on your feet, as one might imagine, but on your hands.
Forbes:	That's right.
Luther:	Why is that?
Forbes:	Do you mean, why am I wearing these skates on my hands instead of on my feet?
Luther:	Exactly.
Forbes:	I don't know how to skate.
Luther:	But it says here that you are in the process of setting a world record for—
Forbes:	*(interrupting)* —for wearing roller skates. Doesn't say anything about feet, does it?
Luther:	No.
Forbes:	I wouldn't have lasted 87 *minutes* with these things on my feet.
Luther:	*(resigned)* And how long have you lasted?
Forbes:	87 days.
Luther:	87 days?
Forbes:	87 days.
Luther:	Certainly is a long time.
Forbes:	I want to set a record that will be hard to break. I plan to keep these skates on until Arbor Day.
Luther:	How long will that make it?
Forbes:	I'm not sure. Actually, I was hoping you could tell me.
Luther:	Tell you what?
Forbes:	When is Arbor Day?
Luther:	*(Pauses to think.)* I'm afraid I don't know. *(another pause)* Perhaps you could visit your local library.
Forbes:	I tried that.
Luther:	And?
Forbes:	They threw me out. Ever try thumbing through a Britannica with roller skates on your hands? I ripped it up good.
Luther:	I bet you've run into a lot of little problems like that.
Forbes:	I sure have. One thing I found rather difficult was eating mashed potatoes.
Luther:	Keep slipping off your wheels, do they?

Forbes: They sure do. And another thing is playing pinochle. Do you know how hard it is to shuffle with these things on?

Luther: *(holding up a hand, signaling Forbes to stop)* I can imagine. *(The voices of the two now begin to overlap as each man continues his own conversation—Luther trying to wrap the show up, Forbes complaining.)*

Forbes: Or making a phone call? Do you know how hard that is? And try explaining to an operator why you're not dialing direct.

Luther: That's fine, thank you, Mr. Forbes.

Forbes: It's nearly impossible.

Luther: Well, thank you for joining us tonight, Mr. Forbes. It certainly was a pleasure.

Forbes: Or playing Ping-Pong?

Luther: *(to audience)* That's all for now, folks. Tune in again next time for more of Put Up or Shut Up.

Forbes: You can't hold a paddle with a roller skate on your hand.

Luther: *(looking offstage)* Are we off? Good.

Forbes: Just try putting some spin on a Ping-Pong ball while you're wearing a roller skate on your hand. *(Luther exits. Forbes follows, still complaining.)*

SENIOR SUPERMAN

This is another interview between our other talk-show host, Abner Theobald Knucklenose the third, and a very old "Superman." Superman should have a cane, be dressed in a ragged, tattered superman suit, and look old and senile.

A.T.K.: This evening, ladies and gentlemen, we have a very special treat for you. We will be interviewing a person whom I am sure all of you will indeed recognize and look up to—that world-renowned man of steel, that man who is faster than a speeding bullet, more powerful than a locomotive, able to leap tall buildings in a single bound. Look—up in the sky! It's a bird, it's a plane—it's Superman! Yes! It's Superman, that strange visitor from another planet who came to earth with powers and abilities far beyond those of mortal men. Superman, who can change the course of mighty rivers and bend steel with his bare hands. And who, disguised as Clark Kent, mild-mannered reporter for a great metropolitan newspaper, fights a neverending battle for truth, justice, and the American way. Ladies and gentlemen, may I introduce to you . . . Superman! *(pause)* Superman! *(pause)* Hey, uh, Sup? Hey, Superman, are you coming? *(Slowly Superman walks out. He is wearing his Clark Kent glasses and hat by mistake.)* Here he is, ladies and gentlemen, Superman himself! *(A.T.K. realizes Superman is wearing his Clark Kent glasses and hat and quickly takes them off him.)*

Superman: Hey, I can't see, ya young whippersnapper. Give me back my glasses! *(A.T.K. whispers to Superman, obviously explaining why he did what he did. Superman gives A.T.K. a big wink and the "high sign" to indicate "O.K.")*

A.T.K.: It certainly is a delight to have you with us this evening, Mr. Superman.
Superman: Yes, it is.

A.T.K.: It is certainly kind of you to come and break away from your busy schedule to be with us.

Superman: Yes, it is.

A.T.K.: Indeed, it is a real thrill for me to personally meet and talk to such a famous person as yourself.

Superman: Yes, it is.

A.T.K.: I'll bet many of our viewers this evening have never had the opportunity to see you in person. I'll bet many would have thought seeing you in person would be disappointing. What do you think?

Superman: Yes, it is.

A.T.K.: Let me direct a few questions your way, Mr. Super.

Superman: Just send 'em slow, fella.

A.T.K.: Certainly. I couldn't help noticing that you walked in and didn't fly. Why is that?

Superman: I don't fly anymore.

A.T.K.: Could I ask why?

Superman: Yes.

A.T.K.: Well?

Superman: Well what?

A.T.K.: Well why?

Superman: Well why what?

A.T.K.: *(louder)* Well, why don't you fly anymore?

Superman: Well, why don't you ask me?

A.T.K.: *(very loud)* O.K., I will—

Superman: *(very soft)* You don't have to holler. I'm sitting right next to you.

A.T.K.: Oh, I'm sorry. *(calmer and softer)* What is the reason you don't fly anymore, Mr. Superman?

Superman: What'd you say?

A.T.K.: *(soft still)* I said, "What is the reason you don't fly anymore, Mr. Super?"

Superman: Speak up, I can't hear you.

A.T.K.: *(upset)* Why don't you fly anymore?

Superman: It's too greasy.

A.T.K.: *(confused)* It's too greasy?

Superman: Yea, and besides I keep burning the bacon.

A.T.K.:   *(more confused)* You keep burning the bacon?

Superman: Yes, you know; when you get older, *fried* foods are too greasy and then I'd turn the heat up too much and burn the bacon.

A.T.K.:   I don't mean "fry," I mean "fly!"

Superman: Oh, why didn't you say so?

A.T.K.:   I did.

Superman: You did what?

A.T.K.:   I did say so.

Superman: You did? I thought you said "fry." *(to audience)* Didn't you think he said "fry?"

A.T.K.:   O.K., O.K. *(very clear and distinct)* Why don't you *fly* anymore?

Superman: Too dangerous.

A.T.K.:   What do you mean, "too dangerous"?

Superman: Let me tell you about the very last time I flew.

A.T.K.:   Yes, please do.

Superman: I was cruising at 20,000 feet, doing about 1200 miles an hour, heading north. I was up there minding my own business when all of a sudden, what's in front of me but a flock of 500 geese heading south for the winter. These were the biggest honkers I'd ever seen. I tried to stop on a dime, but it slid into a quarter, and those geese knocked me to the ground.

A.T.K.:   You really got "down" from a goose, huh? *(Laughs.)*

Superman: Sick! Sick! That's bad! But I never flew again.

A.T.K.:   But you're still a crime fighter, aren't you?

Superman: Oh, yes! Always was, always will be. In fact, I caught me a desperate criminal just last week.

A.T.K.:   You did?

Superman: Yes.

A.T.K.:   Oh, please tell us about it.

Superman: I captured a sixty-eight-year-old lady professional pickpocket.

A.T.K.:   Wow! How did you catch her?

Superman: She tried to pick my pocket, and I don't have any pockets. Hee hee!

A.T.K.:   She sure wasn't very picky to pocket you. What other adventures in crime fighting have recently come your way?

Superman: Well, I'm kept pretty busy defending society from the scum who ignore "No Smoking" signs on public transportation, from jaywalkers, from the villains who don't wash their hands before leaving a public restroom . . . that kind of stuff. But you know, recently, a lot of those criminals have been eluding me.

A.T.K.: Why's that?

Superman: Well, when crime strikes, I can't jump into a phonebooth and change in a second like I used to. It takes at least ten minutes to get out of my Clark Kent outfit and into my superhero uniform. I usually get only halfway through by the time the squad car arrives and takes me in for indecent exposure charges.

A.T.K.: Don't they realize who you are?

Superman: No, and when you're from the planet Krypton, it's difficult to show them the proper identification.

A.T.K.: One thing I am sure our audience would like to know . . .

Superman: (interrupting and getting up to leave) I'm sorry. I must go now.

A.T.K.: But I was just going to ask . . .

Superman: No. No more questions. It's time for my afternoon nap. Got a big game of gin rummy tonight at the Senior Superheroes Home and I've got to be rested.

A.T.K.: Well, ladies and gentlemen, I guess that wraps up our show for tonight. Join us again soon for another of our (Ta-da!) "Famous Interviews."

THE SKYDIVER

You'll need two people for this skit: a "roving reporter" and the skydiver, Rusty Ripcord. . . .

Announcer: Good evening, ladies and gentlemen! This is your roving reporter here at Tonapah, Nevada, covering the world skydiving championships for ABC's Weird World of Sports. Any moment now, the world's leading skydiver, Rusty Ripcord, will be along. (Enter Rusty dressed in a ridiculous outfit: goggles, rope, pack on back, inner tube, pump, combat boots, medals, helmet, tree limb, and so on.)

Rusty: Boy, was that last jump a lulu!

Announcer: Excuse me, Mr. Ripcord—how was your landing?

Rusty:	Well, actually, not so hot. *(Pulls tree limb out of his clothes and tosses it down.)*
Announcer:	Rusty, just how many jumps have you made?
Rusty:	Ninety-five!
Announcer:	Has your chute ever failed to open?
Rusty:	Well, yes, actually—ninety-five times.
Announcer:	Wow, that must be rough!
Rusty:	Not after the first time.
Announcer:	Hey, I can't help but admire your crash helmet.
Rusty:	Thanks. I got it with Betty Crocker coupons. I also got my pants, my car, my house, my wife—
Announcer:	*(interrupting)* Say, what's that medal for?
Rusty:	Oh—that's when I won the First Invitational Indoor Skydiving Championship.
Announcer:	Really? What are all those other medals for?
Rusty:	Well, this one's for twenty-seventh place in the Girl Scout National Championship, and this one is for forty-ninth place, boys five and under.
Announcer:	What about this one? *(Points.)*
Rusty:	That holds my pants up.
Announcer:	Is this your usual attire?
Rusty:	Well, yeah, but it's a little flat right now. *(pointing to inner tube around waist)*
Announcer:	Rusty, what is your specialty?

Rusty: I specialize in diving over great bodies of wat

Announcer: Wow, that's terrific. Are there any particular

Rusty: Yeah, I can't swim.

Announcer: What do you use that inner tube for?

Rusty: Well, it does come in handy as a life raft

Announcer: But how do you inflate it?

Rusty: I just use this tire pump here.

Announcer: Really? How do you hold that pump *demonstrate, but just gets tangled up.)*

Announcer: Rusty, I've heard that most skydivers y do you yell?

Rusty: MOMMY!!!

Announcer: Rusty, when is the best time of ye

Rusty: Anytime but fall.

Announcer: Why not fall?

Rusty: Birds flying south. *(Wipes eyes.*

Announcer: Rusty, would you recommend

Rusty: Skydiving . . . It's the OOONI

Announcer: And now, back to our studic

WHO'S ON FIRST?

This is one of the funniest routines ever done. It originally appeared in an Abbott a ostello film, but it never gets old. The lines by themselves will not carry an audience, so don't read it. The lines *must* be memorized completely—it's impossible to do it any other way. Trying to think it through is much too confusing. Timing is very important. The dialogue must flow, varying in speed and volume, so that the skit climaxes two or three times.

The first man is a sports announcer; the second is the coach of a baseball team. The second guy can be dressed appropriately, with a baseball cap, whistle, and so on.

1st man: I understand you used to coach a baseball team.

2nd man: Yes, I did. It was a pretty good team, in fact.

1st man: Were your players good enough to make the big leagues?

2nd man: Well, yes.

1st man: Hey, why don't you tell us some of their names because they might be famous someday.

2nd man: O.K. Let's see, on the bases we have—Who's on first, What's on second, and I-Don't-Know's on third—

1st man: Wait a minute. You're the manager of the team, aren't you?

2nd man: Yes.

1st man: You're supposed to know all the fellows' names?

2nd man: Of course.

1st man: O.K., then, the first baseman's name.

2nd man: Who.

1st man: The guy on first.

2nd man: Who.

1st man: The *first baseman!*

2nd man: Who is on first base.

1st man: I'm asking *you* who's on first base.

2nd man: That's the man's name.

1st man: That's whose name?

2nd man: Yes.

1st man:	Look, all I want to know is, what's the name of the guy on first base?
2nd man:	No, no—What's on second.
1st man:	Who's on second?
2nd man:	Who's on first.
1st man:	I don't know.
2nd man:	He's on third.
1st man:	Third base? Look—how did we get on third base?
2nd man:	Well, you mentioned the man's name.
1st man:	Whose name?
2nd man:	No, Who is on first.
1st man:	I don't know.
2nd man:	He's on third.
1st man:	Hey, if I mentioned the guy's name, who did I say was on third?
2nd man:	Who is on first.
1st man:	I'm not asking you who's on first . . .
2nd man:	Who *is* on first.
1st man:	I want to know what's the name of the guy on third base.
2nd man:	No. What's on second.
1st man:	Who's on second?
2nd man:	Who's on first.
1st man:	*I don't know!*
Both:	Third base.
1st man:	All right. Just forget the infield. Let's go to the outfield. Do you have a left fielder?
2nd man:	Of course we have a left fielder.
1st man:	The left fielder's name.
2nd man:	Why.
1st man:	Well, I just thought I'd ask.
2nd man:	Well, I just thought I'd tell you.
1st man:	Then go ahead and tell me. What's the left fielder's name?
2nd man:	What's on second.
1st man:	Who's on second?
2nd man:	Who's on first.
1st man:	*I don't know!*

Both:	Third base.
1st man:	Let's try again, The left fielder's name?
2nd man:	Why.
1st man:	Because.
2nd man:	No, he's our center fielder.
1st man:	*(exasperated)* Look. Let's go back to the infield. Do you pay your guys anything?
2nd man:	Yes, as a matter of fact, we give them a little something for uniforms—
1st man:	O.K. Look, it's payday and all the guys are lined up to get paid. The first baseman is standing at the front of the line. Now he reaches out to you to accept his money. Now, who gets the money?
2nd man:	That's right.
1st man:	So who gets the money?
2nd man:	Why not? He's earned it.
1st man:	Who has?
2nd man:	Certainly. Why sometimes even his mother takes the money for him.
1st man:	Whose mother?
2nd man:	Yes.
1st man:	Look. All I am trying to find out is what's the name of your first baseman.
2nd man:	What's on second.
1st man:	Who's on second?
2nd man:	Who's on first.
1st man:	I don't know!
2nd man:	Third base.
1st man:	O.K., O.K., I'll try again. Do you have a pitcher?
2nd man:	Of course we have a pitcher. What kind of team would we be without a pitcher?
1st man:	The pitcher's name?
2nd man:	Tomorrow.
1st man:	What time?
2nd man:	What time what?
1st man:	What time tomorrow are you going to tell me who's pitching?
2nd man:	How many times do I have to tell you? Who is on first.
1st man:	You say *who's on first* one more time and I'll break your arm. I want to know— what's your pitcher's name?

2nd man:	What's on second.
1st man:	Who's on second?
2nd man:	Who's on first.
1st man:	I don't know!
2nd man:	He's on third.
1st man:	The catcher's name?
2nd man:	Today.
1st man:	Today. Tomorrow. What kind of team is this? All right. Let me set up a hypothetical play. Now, Tomorrow's pitching. Today's catching. I am up at bat. Tomorrow pitches to me and I bunt the ball down the first base line. Today being the good catcher that he is, runs down the first base line, picks up the ball and throws it to the first baseman. Now, when he throws the ball to the first baseman, who gets the ball?
2nd man:	That's the first right thing you've said all night.
1st man:	I don't even know what I'm talking about. Look, if he throws the ball to first, somebody has to catch it. So who gets the ball?
2nd man:	Naturally.
1st man:	Who catches it?
2nd man:	Naturally.
1st man:	Ohhhhhh. Today picks up the ball and throws it to Naturally.
2nd man:	He does nothing of the kind. He throws the ball to Who.
1st man:	Naturally.
2nd man:	Right.
1st man:	I just said that. You say it.
2nd man:	He picks up the ball and throws it to Who.
1st man:	Naturally.
2nd man:	That's what I'm saying.
1st man:	Look. Bases are loaded. Somebody gets up to bat and hits a line drive to Who. Who throws to What. What throws to I-Don't-Know. Triple Play! Next batter gets up and hits a long ball to Why. Because? I Don't Know! No, he's on third—and I just don't give a darn!
2nd man:	What?
1st man:	I said I don't give a darn!
2nd man:	Hey, he's our shortstop!

CHAPTER FOUR

THE
CLASSICS

THE FATAL QUEST

This skit requires six characters:
The King
The Devoted Queen
The Handsome Duke
The Lovely Princess
The Curtains (someone with a sign around his neck that says "curtains")
The Kitten

The lines of the script are spoken by each character exactly as they are written. Each character reads his stage directions as a part of his speech, and at the same time suits his actions to his words. Encourage your actors to ham it up, and design appropriate costumes for each character. If possible, have each actor memorize his lines rather than simply read them.

Act One:

Curtain:	The curtain rises for the first act.
Princess:	The fair Princess stands at the window. She hears the distant sound of hoofs. "It is he," she cries, placing her hand upon her beating heart.
King:	Enter the King.
Queen:	Followed by the devoted Queen.
King:	He seats himself on his throne, his scepter in hand.
Queen:	The Queen stands gracefully beside him, gazing at him fondly. "My Lord," she says in gentle tones, "why do you keep the Princess hidden from the eyes of men? Will wedlock never be hers?"
King:	The King waxes stern. "Fair Queen," he says gruffly, "a thousand times have I repeated—the Princess shall become the wife of no man."
Duke:	Enter the handsome Duke. "O King," he says in manly tones, "I have this morning a message of greatest importance."
Princess:	The Princess enters at the left. At the sight of the handsome Duke she is startled. Her embarrassment increases her loveliness.
Duke:	At first glance the Duke falls madly in love.

King:	The King rises in excitement. "Speak," he shouts at the Duke, "and be gone."
Duke:	The Duke gazes at the Princess, his message forgotten.
Princess:	The lovely maiden blushes and drops her eyes.
Queen:	"Daughter," says the Queen, "why do you intrude yourself here without permission?"
Princess:	The Princess opens her mouth to speak.
Duke:	The Duke holds his breath.
Princess:	"Alas," says the maiden in tones melting with sweetness, "my Angora kitten has strayed away and is lost."
Duke:	"Fair Princess," cries the Duke in tones choked with feeling, "service for you were joy. The kitten I swear to find." With high courage he strides away.
King:	"Stop him! Stop him!" shouts the King fiercely. "My servants shall find the cat for the Princess." Exit the King.
Queen:	Followed by the devoted Queen.
Curtain:	The curtain falls.

Act Two:

Curtain:	The curtain rises for the second act.
Princess:	The fair Princess stands at the window. She hears the distant sound of hoofs. "It is he," she cries, placing her hand upon her beating heart.
King:	Enter the King.
Queen:	Followed by the devoted Queen.
Duke:	The Duke steps in buoyantly, puss in arms.
Princess:	"My kitten, my kitten," cries the Princess joyously. She takes her pet in her arms, but her eyes follow the stalwart form of the Duke.
King:	The King is pierced with jealousy.
Duke:	The Duke falls upon his knees before the King. "O King," he says manfully, "I have found the kitten! I have come to claim the reward . . . the hand of the Princess."
King:	The King trembles with wrath. "Be gone," he shouts furiously. "The hand of the Princess shall be won by no cat."

Duke:	The Duke departs. As he passes the Princess, he grasps her soft hand. "I will return," he whispers in her ear.
Princess:	The Princess does not speak, but her clear blue eyes reflect the secret of her soul.
Curtain:	The curtain falls.

Act Three:

Curtain:	The curtain rises for the third and fatal act.
King:	The King stands morosely in the center of the stage.
Queen:	The Queen stands sadly beside him. "My Lord," she says in pleading tones, "relent. The Princess weeps day and night, nor will she be comforted."
King:	The King turns his back. "Hold your peace!" he says in harsh tones.
Queen:	The Queen weeps.
Duke:	Enter the Duke, his sword at his side. "Oh, King," he says in white passion, "for the last time I ask you for the hand of your daughter."
King:	The King spurns him. "Be gone," he shouts once more.
Duke:	The Duke draws his sword and stabs the King.
King:	The King gasps and dies.
Queen:	"My Lord, my Lord," cries the Queen passionately, and she falls dead upon the King.
Duke:	"Great Caesar's Ghost, what have I done!" cries the Duke in anguish. He drinks a cup of poison and falls dead.
Princess:	Hearing the cry, the Princess enters. She stops transfixed at the horrible sight before her. "Heaven help me," she cries, waving her shapely arms. "I die of grief." She falls dead upon the breast of her beloved.
King:	Wee, wee, the King of the Land is dead.
Queen:	Alas, alas, the devoted Queen is dead.
Duke:	The Duke, remorseful beyond bearing, joins them in death.
Princess:	The Princess is dead, and beautiful even in death.
Curtain:	The curtain falls.

Postlude:

Curtain:	The curtain rises for the postlude.

King:	The King is still dead.
Duke:	The manly Duke is still dead.
Queen:	The devoted Queen is still dead.
Princess:	The beautiful Princess is still dead and still beloved.
Curtain:	The curtain falls forever.

FRONTIER MORTICIAN

This skit has been around for more than two decades and it is still one of the funniest. It is loaded with one-liners and puns that have become classics over the years.

Characters:

The Announcer
Sam Alamode
Piney ("Pie") Alamode
Trigger Mortis ("Trig")
Joe Silver
Arnie

Announcer: The makers of Fatrical present *(music)* FRONTIER MORTICIAN! Are you skinny and run down? Are you so thin you have to wear skis in the bathtub to keep from going down the drain? When you turn sideways and stick out your tongue, do you look like a zipper? When you drink strawberry pop, do you look like a thermometer? Then you need Fatrical—the drink that adds weight to you. Fatrical is not a capsule, it is not a solid, it is not a liquid—it's a gas that you inhale. Fatrical comes in one delicious gas flavor—mustard. It costs only $4.95 a case, and the equipment for inhaling it costs only $5,678. This includes a 5,000-cubic-foot tank, 400 feet of hose, three pumps, two filter tips, and a partridge in a pear tree. Now for our story—The Adventures of Trigger Mortis, Frontier Mortician. The scene opens in the residence of Sam Alamode, wealthy rancher and owner of the Bar-B-Q ranch in Sparerib, Texas. Sam is dying and is talking to his lovely daughter Piney Alamode, whom he lovingly calls Pie. . . .

Sam:	Pie, honey, I'm dying again. Go call Trigger Mortis, the frontier mortician. Have hearse will travel.
Pie:	What's wrong with you, Daddy? What's your ailment?
Sam:	I swallowed the thermometer and I'm dying by degrees.
Pie:	I'll go call Trigger Mortis right now!
Announcer:	Unknown to Sam Alamode, his head foreman, Joe Silver, is hiding outside listening to the conversation. He's a full-blooded Indian, and Sam always calls him his faithful Indian companion Silver. Sam doesn't hear Joe speak.
Joe:	Let old Sam die. I wish he would. Then I can get the ranch and be set for life. He's always got some fool disease. Last week he swallowed a dynamite cap and his hair came out in bangs. Before that he swallowed a hydrogen bomb and had atomic ache. He's suffering from flower disease—he's a blooming idiot. Hey— here comes Pie Alamode's stupid boyfriend, Arnie. Poor kid—he's an orphan. Little orphan Arnie. I'll just sneak away.
Arnie:	I haven't seen my girlfriend Pie Alamode for two weeks. Boy, she has lovely eyes—one is brown and other two are blue. Last time I was here she rolled her eyes at me, and I picked them up and rolled them back. I remember the first time she kissed me—it made chills go up and down my spine. Then I found out her Popsicle was leaking. I'll knock at the door. *(Knocks.)*
Pie:	Who is it?
Arnie:	It's me, honey—and I call you honey cause you have hives.
Pie:	Oh, my cookie—and I call you cookie because you're so crummy.
Announcer:	We interrupt this love scene to bring you a message from Peter Pan makeup. Use Peter Pan before your pan peters out. This is the makeup used by the stars— Lassie, Gentle Ben, Phyllis Diller. Listen to this letter from Mrs. Mergatroid Fluglehorn from Liverlip, Mississippi: "My face was so wrinkled I had to screw my hat on. Then I used Peter Pan makeup and I don't look like an old woman anymore—I look like an old man. I had my wrinkles tightened up, and now every time I raise my eyebrows, I pull up my socks. I give all the credit to Peter Pan." Use Peter Pan, and you can be beautiful, too. Now, back to Frontier Mortician—Trigger Mortis, the frontier mortician, is answering his telephone.
Trig:	Oh, it's you, Miss Pie Alamode. You want me to come to see your father? Well, my hearse has been giving me trouble—I think I blew a casket. I've got to quit

	using embalming fluid in the gas tank—the motor keeps dying. Yes . . . yes . . . well, I have to finish my breakfast. I'm eating Shrouded Wheat and Ghost Toasties. . . . Well, I'll hurry right out. Goodbye—I must be shoveling off.
Announcer:	Pie Alamode hangs up and goes to meet her lover, little orphan Arnie, in their favorite meeting place . . . the family graveyard.
Pie:	It's so romantic here in the graveyard. There's the grave of my Uncle Earnest. Look . . . there are some maggots making love in dead earnest.
Arnie:	Darling, may I have your hand in marriage?
Pie:	My hand? Oh, yes. In fact, you can have my arm, too.
Arnie:	Here, I'll put this ring on your finger.
Pie:	Awwww, your face is turning red.
Arnie:	Yeah, and your finger's turning green. After all, we've been going together for twelve years now.
Pie:	So what do you want—a pension? Let's go tell my father.
Announcer:	This program is brought to you by the Double Insanity Insurance Company. Mothers, do you have children? Then protect them with a double deal policy. We pay $100,000 if your son is killed by a herd of white elephants going east on Thursday. If you lose an arm, we help you look for it. If you get hit in the head, we pay you in one lump sum. We have a double indemnity clause, too—if you die in an accident, we bury you twice. Now, a report from the National Safety Council. It is predicted that 356 people will die in accidents this weekend. So far only 135 have been reported. Some of you aren't trying. Now, back to our story. Joe Silver is plotting to kidnap Pie Alamode and hold her for ransom. He thinks Sam Alamode is dying, but he really isn't. Trigger Mortis, frontier mortician, is on his way to the ranch.
Trig:	Well, here I am. When you're at death's door, I'll pull you through.
Sam:	Good to see you, Trigger. Can you give me a good funeral?
Trig:	I'll give you a good funeral or your mummy back. Could I interest you in our new layaway plan?
Sam:	I'm a sick man, a sick man. The doctor told me to drink some medicine after a hot bath, and I could hardly finish drinking the bath.
Trig:	You need some of my Whistler's Mother medicine—one dose and you're off your rocker.

Sam:	Trigger, I can trust you, can't I?
Trig:	Of corpse, of corpse. Have I ever let you down?
Sam:	I don't trust my faithful Indian companion, Silver. He has a sneaky look.
Trig:	I happen to know, Sam, that Joe Silver wants to kidnap your daughter and keep her from marrying little orphan Arnie.
Sam:	Trigger, we gotta do something. Think of a plan.
Announcer:	Will Trigger Mortis think of a plan? While he thinks, a word from Honest John Pendergast, the used car dealer. Honest John has bargains in used cars that you can't afford to miss. Here's an 1887 Essex—this is a revolutionary car— Washington drove it at Valley Forge. The tires are so beat that you not only knock the pedestrians down, you whip them to death. This car has low lines—in fact, it's so low it doesn't have doors—it has manhole covers. This program is also brought to you by Glum, the toothpaste that gives your bad breath the Good Housekeeping seal of approval. Are your teeth like the Ten Commandments—all broken? Do you have a Pullman-car mouth—one upper and one lower? Then use Glum. Glum contains eucalyptus oil, flown in from Australia. This eucalyptus oil is the secret of Glum. Millions of users say, "Man, you clipt us." Be true to your teeth and they will never be false to you. Now, back to Frontier Mortician. Sam, Pie, Arnie, and Trigger Mortis are trying to figure out how to get rid of Joe Silver.
Sam:	I have a splitting headache.
Trig:	Have your eyes ever been checked?
Sam:	No, they've always been blue. Trigger, why don't we put Joe in one of your coffins and ship him out of the state?
Trig:	A tisket, a tasket, I'll put him in a casket. Listen, Sam—I was in love once, so I know what Arnie and Pie are going through.
Pie:	You were in love?
Trig:	I was stuck on a girl who worked in the glue factory. She had a schoolgirl complexion—with diplomas under her eyes. Her lips were like petals—bicycle pedals. Those lips . . . those teeth . . . that hair . . . that eye . . .
Arnie:	Hey—here comes Joe Silver. Get your coffin ready, Trigger.
Pie:	Daddy, lie on the bed and act like you're dead.

Announcer:	Sam lies on the bed and holds his breath. Trigger takes off his shoes and they all hold their breath. At this breathless moment, we bring you the daily police calls. Calling car 15, calling car 15—happy birthday, car 15, you are now car 16. Car 56, car 56, rush to the Bungling Brothers' Circus. The fat woman has hay fever and is crying so much three midgets are about to drown. Car 23, car 23—return the 10-gallon hat bought for the mayor—he has an 11-gallon head. Car 19, go to the corner of 6th and Main—the Chinese cook has just committed chop sueycide. Now, back to the story. Joe Silver enters Sam's bedroom as the others hide.
Joe:	So I finally caught you, you scoundrel. You've cut my check so many times I have to endorse it with Mercurochrome. I want to marry your daughter, Sam, and nobody's gonna stop me. Sure I'm tough—I've been sent up the river so many times I get fan mail from the salmon. The last time they caught me I got ten years in jail and two in the electric chair. Even when I was a baby people were pinning things on me. Now, I'm gonna get you.
Sam:	Get him, Arnie!
Trig:	Quick, I have the casket opened. Push him, Arnie!
Joe:	Help—help—you're pushing me . . . (muffled sounds)
Trig:	That takes care of him. Now I have to run for a body. A fellow in town swallowed a quart of shellac and died. He had a lovely finish.
Arnie:	How can we thank you? You'll come to the wedding, won't you?
Trig:	Yes, I plan to give you a tombstone for a present, but don't take it for granite.
Sam:	Thanks, Trig. By the way, stop over and we'll play golf someday.
Trig:	Don't ever play golf with an undertaker—he's always on top at the last hole. (Sam and Trig exit.)
Arnie:	Now we're alone, Pie, my love. Someday you'll have my name.
Pie:	I never did find out—what is your last name, Arnie?
Arnie:	My name is Arnie R. Square.
Pie:	What a lovely name I'll have—Mrs. Pie R. Square.
Ann:	And as the sun sinks slowly in the west, we leave the lovers as they plan their future. Tune in tomorrow for a new adventure, brought to you by Bleeties, the cereal for old goats. Bleeties contains 56% iron, 22% copper, 78% steel, 14% bronze, and 11% zinc. It doesn't snap, crackle, or pop—it lies there and rusts.

Bleeties isn't the breakfast of champions—it's for people who just want to get into the semifinals. In closing, be sure to visit your local dime store where they're having a monster sale. Haven't you always wanted to own your own monster? We have vampires at special prices. They're excellent for curing tired blood! These are experienced vampires who all worked as tellers in blood banks. Now—tune in tomorrow for the first episode of the new story, "I was a Teenage Spinster," brought to you by the gardener's magazine, Weeder's Digest.

FRONTIER PSYCHIATRIST

You'll need nine people for this skit:
The Announcer
Dr. Tex Rorschach (*pronounced 'roar-shock'*), the Frontier Psychiatrist
The Nurse
The Sheriff
Ringo Kid
Buck

The Bartender
The Friend

Scene One:

The skit opens in the office of Dr. Rorschach.

Doctor:	*(talking on phone)* And so, madam, I want you to go back to the reservation and tell your husband that he can walk if he wants to. It's all in his mind, purely psychosomatic. Your husband can walk if he wants to. Well, goodbye, Mrs. Sitting Bull. *(Hangs up.)*
	An interesting case. She can use a little treatment too. She's got a forty-pound papoose on her back. Oh, nurse!
Nurse:	Yes, Doctor Rorschach?
Doctor:	Any more appointments today?
Nurse:	Let's see—Ben Cartwright at 3:00. Roy Rogers at 4:00. Matt Dillon is coming in at 5:00. The Lone Ranger at 6:00.
Doctor:	Ah, ha, ha. The Lone Ranger. Very interesting case! Acute paranoia. Persecution complex. He thinks the C.I.A. is trying to see what he looks like under his mask. Eh—now, nurse, I want you to . . . *(gunshots)*
Doctor:	What the . . .
Sheriff:	Doctor, doctor!
Doctor:	Oh, hello, sheriff. You're just in time for your appointment. Come in and lie down on the couch and—
Sheriff:	No time, Doc—we're in for a pack of trouble! The Ringo Kid just pulled into town.
Doctor:	The Ringo Kid?
Sheriff:	Yeah! The dirtiest, rottenest killer north of the Rio Grande. Why, he's a murdering outlaw—
Doctor:	Please, sheriff—how many times do I have to tell you, there are no such things as outlaws. Just problem cowboys!
Sheriff:	I tell you, he's a killer! He came into town this morning and shot my deputy.
Doctor:	Now, just a minute, I just saw your deputy and talked to him.

Sheriff:	Did he answer you?
Doctor:	Come to think of it, no. I thought it was some kind of mental block.
Sheriff:	Well, I'm telling you, Doc— *(shots and yelling offstage)*
Sheriff:	Galloping coyotes! It's Buck! He's been shot!
Buck:	He got me! The Ringo Kid got me! *(Coughs.)*
Doctor:	Oh, you've got to do something about that cough, Buck. You know, really, it's just nerves. Nerves, you know. Just nerves.
Sheriff:	Where is he now, Buck?
Buck:	He's in the saloon. *(Coughs.)*
Doctor:	Maybe it's heartburn. Are you a compulsive eater? Now just lie down here and start at the beginning and tell me whatever comes to mind. First, what do you think about girls—
Sheriff:	No, no, no, Doc! He's been shot, and the Ringo Kid did it.
Doctor:	Oh! Well, I'll go into the saloon after him. Excuse me . . .
Sheriff:	Wait a minute, Doc! That's dangerous.
Doctor:	Sheriff! I am a frontier psychiatrist and that boy needs therapy. Nurse! Where's my notebook and pencil?
Nurse:	In your holster.
Doctor:	Oh, yeah.
Sheriff:	But, Doc—you can't go in there. I tell you, he's vicious.
Doctor:	He's *not* vicious.
Sheriff:	Well, what would make a man shoot people in the back?
Doctor:	Poor toilet training? Who knows. Now if you'll excuse me, please . . .
Nurse:	Be careful, doctor. Oh, please be careful. You know how I feel about you.
Doctor:	I told you before, nurse, I'm just your father image. Now go finish the slipcovers for the couch please.

Scene Two:

In the saloon. Piano is playing. Shots offstage—Ringo enters—people scream.

Ringo:	All right—now, listen to me. I'm the Ringo Kid. I'm the shootingest, fightingest hombre in the West. Anybody want to take me on?

Men:	*(as a group)* No, No, No!
Ringo:	All right, I'll tell you what. Line up, you guys. Now when I count three, you go for your guns.

(Guys line up—Ringo shoots them—they drop.)

Ringo:	One, two, three. Ya gotta be quicker than that. Ha, ha, ha, ha, ha, ha, ha. Hey, did you see that, stranger?
Stranger:	Yeah!
Ringo:	*(Bang!)* I don't like witnesses. All right, piano player, let's have a tune. *(Piano plays, then stops suddenly as doctor enters.)*
Doctor:	Howdy, Ringo Kid.
Ringo:	Who are you?
Doctor:	*(Walks up.)* Doctor Tex Rorschach, frontier psychiatrist. Have couch will travel.
Ringo:	What?
Doctor:	Now, what seems to be your problem?
Ringo:	Problem? I gotta itchy trigger finger, Doc.
Doctor:	Oh! That's not my field. Try a dermatologist.
Ringo:	*Wait a minute*—just what do you want?
Doctor:	I want to help you!
Ringo:	Aha! I got you figured. Just a cheap analyst trying to make a reputation. Awright, start dancing, head shrinker! *(Points gun and shoots.)*
Doctor:	Poor Ringo Kid. You're just an angry little boy lashing out at the world with your six-gun. Hmm Hmmm.
Ringo:	I'm gonna kill you.
Doctor:	Oho! A textbook case. Ha-ha! Wait till I write the boys in Vienna. They'll flip.
Ringo:	Awright, you asked for it. *(Points gun—shoots.)*
Doctor:	You're insecure, aren't you?
Ringo:	What?
Doctor:	You're full of frustration and aggressive hostilities—it's all an artificial barrier to mask your inhibitions and your massive inferiority complex.
Ringo:	You trying to tell me I'm crazy?

Doctor:	Oh, please, Ringo—we don't use words like crazy anymore. Let me simply say that you're suffering from a traumatic dislocation of your emotional processes.
Ringo:	Well, what does that mean?
Doctor:	You're a fruitcake! You're crazy in the coconut!
Ringo:	Awright.
Doctor:	You're *machuga!!*
Ringo:	Awright, awright, you can talk to my gun.
Doctor:	Ha, ha, ha—that's not a gun.
Ringo:	It isn't?
Doctor:	Of course not. It's a symbol.
Ringo:	A symbol?
Doctor:	A symbol of your inability to cope with reality. Now give me that symbol.
Ringo:	A symbol? *(Hands it over.)*
Doctor:	Now the other symbol.
Ringo:	Here.
Doctor:	Hmmm. You're a good man, Ringo, and I can bring out that goodness.
Ringo:	Ya, ya, ya can?
Doctor:	All you have to do is talk it out. Now lie down on the bar.
Ringo:	Uh, all right, Doc. *(Organ music cuts in.)*
Doctor:	Now, tell me, Ringo—when did you first discover you hated your horse?
Ringo:	But I don't hate my horse.
Doctor:	Ah! Well, does your horse hate you?
Ringo:	Why should my horse hate me?
Doctor:	Well, you sit on him, you make him live in a stable, you feed him oats. Don't you think it logical that the beast should harbor some resentment?
Ringo:	Well, I, I guess so.
Doctor:	Did anything unusual happen to you as a child?
Ringo:	Well, let me think. Oh, yeah! Yeah! When I was eight years old, my home ran away from me.
Doctor:	You mean, you ran away from home?
Ringo:	No, my home ran away from me. We lived in a covered wagon and I fell out.
Doctor:	Aha!! Ringola, Tringola—I think I have solved your problem. Your hostility to everyone is a minification of rejection. You have hallucinations that people

don't like you and that is why you shoot them. If you act friendly to them, they will act friendly to you.

Ringo:	You mean, if I like them they're gonna like me?
Doctor:	Siggy Freud couldn't have put it better.
Ringo:	Doc! How can I ever thank you?
Doctor:	You can pay me. I don't want to feel rejected.
Ringo:	From now on I'm gonna love everybody.
Doctor:	That's it!
Ringo:	Hello, bartender, glad to see ya!
Bartender:	Howdy!
Ringo:	Hey there, friend—pleased to meetcha!
Friend:	Oh! How're you?
Ringo:	Hey! Here comes the sheriff. Hello there, sheriff—glad to see you. *(Sheriff shoots Ringo.)*
Doctor:	Sheriff, why did you shoot that well-adjusted cowpoke?
Sheriff:	I don't know. I just shot him. Something came over me, Doc!
Doctor:	I see. Give me that symbol.
Sheriff:	Here you are.
Doctor:	Now lie down on the bar.
Sheriff:	Ahhhh.
Doctor:	Now tell me, when did you first discover you hated your horse? *(Organ music comes in.)*
Sheriff:	I don't hate my horse.
Doctor:	Well, then, does your horse hate you? *(curtain)*

RINSE THE BLOOD OFF MY TOGA

This skit is a takeoff on Shakespeare's *Julius Caesar*. It's one of the real classic skits and should be carefully learned and rehearsed before presentation. Choose your sets, props, and costumes creatively, remembering that the dialogue will usually carry the skit without elaborate props.

Characters:

Flavius Maximus
Secretary
Brutus
Calpurnia
Senators (three or four will do)
Mark Antony
Claudius
Tiberius
Sergeant

THE SCENE: Rome—44 B.C.

Flavius:	*(to audience)* My name is Flavius Maximus. I'm a private Roman eye. My license number is IXIVLLCCDIXMB. Also comes in handy as an eye chart. Tonight, I'm going to tell you about the Julius Caesar caper. It all began during the Ides of March. I was in my office. I'd just sent another criminal to jail—Sutonius, the Gladiator. He'd been fixing fights at the Coliseum. Had a crooked lion that kept taking a dive. As I was sitting there, my secretary walked in.
Secretary:	Good morning, Flavius. Here's the mail.
Flavius:	Easy with those marble postcards. Break my table. Anything else, babe?
Secretary:	Yeah. There's somebody outside to see you. Seems awfully excited about something.
Flavius:	O.K. Show him in, doll.
Secretary:	Would you come in, sir?
Brutus:	Thank you, miss. You Flavius Maximus, private Roman eye?
Flavius:	Yeah. What's on your mind?
Brutus:	Are you sure we're alone?
Flavius:	I'm sure we're alone.
Brutus:	Well, who's that standing beside you?
Flavius:	That's you, stupid. *(to audience)* I could see I was dealing with no ordinary man. This guy was a nut. *(to Brutus)* O.K., what's on your mind?

Brutus:	Flavius Maximus, a terrible thing has happened. It's the greatest crime in the history of Rome.
Flavius:	Awright, give it to me straight. What's up?
Brutus:	Julius Caesar has been murdered!
Flavius:	*(to audience)* Julius Caesar murdered! I couldn't believe my ears. Big Juli was dead.
Brutus:	Yeah, he was killed just twenty minutes ago. It happened in the Senate. He was stabbed.
Flavius:	Stabbed?
Brutus:	Yeah, they got him right in the rotunda!
Flavius:	Ow, that's a painful spot. I had a splinter there once.
Brutus:	Yeah.
Flavius:	Those marble splinters, you know.
Brutus:	I tell you, Flavius, all of Rome is in an uproar. I came to you because you're the top private eye in Rome. You've got to find the killer.
Flavius:	Well *(pleased)*, I'll try.
Brutus:	You can do it! After all, you're the guy who got Nero. You sent him up on that arson rap.
Flavius:	Oh, yeah, Nero. The whole town was burnt up about him, eh? *(Laughs.)* You get it? The whole town—Jupiter!
Brutus:	What do you say, Flavius? Will you take the case?
Flavius:	Just a minute, pally. I like to know who I'm working for. Just who are you?
Brutus:	I'm a senator. I was Caesar's best friend. The name's Brutus.
Flavius:	Brutus, eh? All right, Brutus, you got yourself a boy. I'll take the case. My fee is 125 drachmas a day—payable in advance.
Brutus:	O.K. Here. *(Pours coins in Flavius's hand.)*
Flavius:	You're one short.
Brutus:	Hey, you got a good ear.
Flavius:	When it comes to money, perfect pitch. Let's go, eh? *(to audience)* We went outside, flagged a passing chariot, and made our way down the Via Appia. The streets were crowded with the usual people—slaves, legionnaires, patricians, and little men who came out of doorways and sold you postcards from Gaul. Before long we found ourselves at the Senate. *(sounds of men in Senate)*

Brutus:	Well, Flavius, this is where it happened. This is where Big Juli got knocked off.
Flavius:	Yeah. Now where's the corpus delicti?
Brutus:	The what?
Flavius:	The corpus delicti. What's the matter, don't you understand plain Latin? The body!
Brutus:	Oh, the stiff.
Flavius:	Yeah.
Brutus:	Right over there.
Flavius:	Wowee! Eight daggers in him.
Brutus:	Yeah, what do you think?
Flavius:	If he were alive today he'd be a pretty sick boy!
Brutus:	Yeah.
Flavius:	He's really fixed for blades, eh? *(Laughs.)*
Brutus:	Aw, come on, Flavius. You gotta solve this crime.
Flavius:	Awright, awright. Fill me in on the set-up here. Now who are those guys over there?
Brutus:	They were all here when it happened. That's Publius; that's Casca; there's Tribonius.
Flavius:	I see. Who's that guy over there with the lean and hungry look on his kisser?
Brutus:	That's Cassius.
Flavius:	Looks like a loser from the Coliseum. Now, who do you think is the likeliest suspect?
Brutus:	That fellow next to him.
Flavius:	Wait a minute—that's you.
Brutus:	I know, but can I be trusted?
Flavius:	*(to audience)* I could see I was dealing with no ordinary case. This was a mental case. *(sound of walking)* Wait a minute. Who's the dame?
Brutus:	Caesar's wife. Name's Calpurnia.
Flavius:	Yeah, well—she's a suspect.
Brutus:	Sure.
Flavius:	Just a minute, Pardon me. Uh—Mrs. Caesar?
Calpurnia:	Yes?

Flavius:	Flavius Maximus, private Roman eye. I'd like to ask you a few questions. What do you know about this?
Calpurnia:	I told him. I told him, "Juli, don't go."
Flavius:	What?
Calpurnia:	"Juli, don't go," I told him. No, he wouldn't listen to me.
Flavius:	Now, look, Mrs. Caesar, I—
Calpurnia:	If I told him once, I told him a thousand times, "Juli don't go . . ."
Flavius:	Don't get upset, ma'am—
Calpurnia:	I begged him, "Juli, don't go." I said, "It's the Ides of March. Beware, already."
Flavius:	Yeah.
Calpurnia:	But would he listen to his wife? No!
Flavius:	Awright, take it easy. Sergeant, you want to take Mrs. Caesar home, please?
Sergeant:	Come along, ma'am. Come along.
Calpurnia:	I told him, "Juli, don't go." *(fade out)* I told him, "Juli, don't go."
Flavius:	*(to audience)* I don't blame him for going! All right, you senators. You can go too, but don't leave town. *(Senators grumble as they leave.)*
Brutus:	Well, what do you think?
Flavius:	I don't know! Not an angle anywhere. Not a clue.
Brutus:	Well, cheer up, Flavius. After all, Rome wasn't built in a day.
Flavius:	Hey—wha'd you say?
Brutus:	I said, "Rome wasn't built in a day."
Flavius:	That's good. "Rome wasn't built in a day." That's *very* good.
Brutus:	You like it?
Flavius:	Yeah.
Brutus:	It's yours.
Flavius:	Thanks. Well, let's reconstruct the crime. Now, Caesar was over there and—
Brutus:	Right over here, yeah.
Flavius:	Hst.
Brutus:	What's the matter?
Flavius:	*(softly)* Somebody's behind that pillar. I'll go get him. Hsh. *(pause)* Awright buddy. Come on out. What are you doin' hangin' around here?
Mark:	Why shouldn't I? I'm Mark Antony.
Flavius:	Mark Antony?

Mark:	Yeah, I just made a speech over the body of Caesar. I said, "Friends, Romans, countrymen, lend me your ears!"
Flavius:	Yeah? What you got in that sack?
Mark:	Ears!
Flavius:	Get out of here!
Mark:	Wait a minute. Don't you want to know who bumped off Julius Caesar?
Flavius:	Yeah. You know who did it?
Mark:	His name is *(dies in agony)* ahh—oooooo—eeeee—ohhhhh—ahhhhh.
Flavius:	That's a funny name. Must be Greek.
Brutus:	No. Look! He's dead.
Flavius:	*(to audience)* What a case. All I got for clues is two dead bodies and a sackful of ears.
Brutus:	Now, look, Flavius—I'm paying you 100 drachmas a day to solve this case.
Flavius:	125 drachmas.
Brutus:	That's right. You got a good ear.
Flavius:	I got a *sackful* of good ears.
Brutus:	Now look—let's have some action here, eh?
Flavius:	Awright, awright. Don't get your toga in a knot. Listen, I got a pal.
Brutus:	Yeah?
Flavius:	Claudius. Runs a bar on the Via Flaminia. He should have a few answers.
Brutus:	That's the idea. Get out among the people, ask questions. After all, when in Rome, do as the Romans do.
Flavius:	Hey—what was that one?
Brutus:	I said, "When in Rome, do as the Romans do."
Flavius:	Oh—that's very good. "When in Rome, do as the Romans do."
Brutus:	You like it?
Flavius:	Yeah.
Brutus:	It's yours.
Flavius:	Thanks. I'll see you later. *(to audience)* Claudius's bar and grill is a hangout where I get answers. It's just a small place with a few tables and a guy in the corner playin' a cool reed pipe.
Claudius:	Hi ya, Flav.
Flavius:	Hi, Claud. What's new?

Claudius:	Nothing much. What ya drinkin'?
Flavius:	Give me a martinus.
Claudius:	You mean a martini.
Flavius:	If I want two, I'll ask for 'em. Look, I'm working on this Julius Caesar kill. You know anything?
Claudius:	Try that dame over there.
Flavius:	Yeah?
Claudius:	Yeah.
Flavius:	Awright, sister, start talkin'.
Calpurnia:	I told him, "Juli, don't go!"
Flavius:	Oh, no!
Calpurnia:	"Juli, don't go . . ."
Flavius:	Get out of here! Hsheeee!
Claudius:	Hey, look, uh—Flavius. I, uh, think I know the guy you're looking for.
Flavius:	You mean Mr. Big?
Claudius:	Yeah. His name is *(dies in agony)* ooooo—eeeeeee—aaaaaaaa—eeeeeeeeeeeeg.
Flavius:	That's an interesting name. Got a chisel? I'd like to write that down. Claudius! Claudius! *(to audience)* I would never get any more conversation out of him. He was dead. This was shapin' up bigger than I thought. Suddenly I looked up. There was Brutus.
Brutus:	Hello, Flavius.
Flavius:	Brutus, what are you doing here?
Brutus:	Hey, I was lookin' for you. Who's that on the floor?
Flavius:	Claudius, the bartender.
Brutus:	Funny place to carry a knife—in his back.
Flavius:	He's dead. He was stabbed—through the portico.
Brutus:	Man, that's even more painful than the rotunda.
Flavius:	Yeah.
Brutus:	Well, have you come up with any answers? Who killed Julius Caesar?
Flavius:	*(to audience)* I started to think, and slowly the pieces fell into place. Brutus was the only man around when all those guys got killed—Caesar, Antony, the bartender—Brutus was always there. Things were beginning to add up. I put two and two together and it came out IV. It was time to make my move!

Brutus:	What do you mean IV?
Flavius:	Four, stupid.
Brutus:	Well, have you come up with any answers? Who killed Julius Caesar?
Flavius:	Only one guy coulda done it.
Brutus:	Yeah? Who?
Flavius:	Let's not play games, Brutus. Or should I say—Mr. Big!
Brutus:	What are you gettin' at?
Flavius:	If the sandal fits, wear it. You knocked off Big Juli!
Brutus:	Ha! You're out of your head. I hired you to find the killer.
Flavius:	Pretty smart, but not smart enough! Awright—you gonna talk, or do I have to call in a couple of centurions to lean on ya?
Brutus:	All right, flatfoot. I did it. I admit it. I knocked off Big Juli, and I'd do it again.
Flavius:	That's all I want to know. I'm sendin' you up the Tiber for a long stretch. Come on, I'll call a chariot, and we'll go downtown.
Brutus:	Don't move unless you want a dagger in the toga.
Flavius:	What?
Brutus:	I'm gettin' out of here. Don't try to stop me!
Flavius:	(to audience) He had the drop on me and I couldn't stop him, but I knew where he was heading. For the scene of the crime—the Senate. And fifteen minutes later I pulled up in my chariot. Tiberius! Tiberius, hand me the ram's horn . . .
Tiberius:	Here you are, Flav.
Flavius:	(Cups hands over mouth.) Awright Brutus. This is Flavius Maximus. I know you're in there. Now, come out with your hands up!
Brutus:	Hang it on your nose, you dirty rotten flatfoot! Come in and get me!
Flavius:	Get smart, Brutus. We can smoke you out. We'll throw incense. We'll throw in an onion on a spear!
Brutus:	I don't care what you do!
Flavius:	Awright, you asked for it! Give it to him, Tiberius! (sound of breaking glass, yelling, and talking) O.K., Brutus, one false move and I'll fill ya full of bronze!
Brutus:	All right, you got me, you creep. But I'll be back!
Flavius:	Oh, no, you won't. This isn't a series.
Brutus:	What?

Flavius:	It's just one little Halloween party. *(or whatever event it is you're performing this skit for)*
Brutus:	Don't worry, I'll be back. Just remember: "All roads lead to Rome."
Sergeant:	Come on, you.
Flavius:	Hey, wait! Bring him back!
Brutus:	What?
Flavius:	That one was a dandy!
Brutus:	What are you talking about?
Flavius:	"All roads lead to Rome." That's good, you know that?
Brutus:	Like it?
Flavius:	Yeah.
Brutus:	Well, you can't have it.
Flavius:	Get out of here!
Man:	Good work, Flavius. All Rome salutes you. Hail, Flavius!
All:	Hail, Flavius!
Flavius:	Thanks, boys. Now if you don't mind, I've got a date with a doll. O.K., baby, I'm ready. You sure your husband doesn't mind?
Girl:	Frankly, I don't care. I told him, "Juli, don't go—"
Flavius:	Oh, no.
Girl:	"Juli, don't go," I told him . . . *(fade out)*

CHAPTER FIVE

STUNTS

BUCKET TRICK

This is a stunt you play on the entire group. You need one helper. Announce that you have a bucket of water from the fountain of youth. (Or any story you want to make up.) Ask for a volunteer—and choose your clued-in helper. The bucket is brought in. Be sure the audience can't see inside it, because it's really a bucket of rice or confetti with a dipper sticking out of it. Inside the dipper is some water. The outside of the dipper must be dry so that no rice will stick to it. You take the dipper out of the bucket, pour the water into a glass, and the volunteer drinks it. He waits, starts acting like a two-year-old, grabs the bucket, and throws its contents all over the audience.

BUZZ, BUZZ, LITTLE BEE

Introduce this by explaining to the group that you're going to give a lesson on the facts of life—"the birds and the bees." But, due to a lack of time, you'll only have time to cover the "bees" part.

Next, choose a volunteer from the group—someone you know is a good sport and will play along with some enthusiasm. Seat him in a chair at the front of the room, facing the group. Explain to him that he is to pretend that the room is a garden, and the stage area is the beehive, and that he is the queen bee, the ruler of the hive. You are the worker bee. Now, explaining as you go, go out into the garden and gather the pollen and bring it back to the hive. (When you go out into the group, you should use your arms like wings, buzz a lot, and make this a fun thing to watch.) When you return to the beehive with your load of pollen, you will say (in bee language), "Whompf!" The queen bee (your volunteer) must say it back: "Whompf!" Have him practice it a few times, and when he does it good and loud, have the group applaud.

Then go out into the garden again and gather a second load of pollen. When you return to the hive with your second load, you say, "Whompf! Whompf!" The queen bee must say it back: "Whompf! Whompf!"

Now—explain to your volunteer that, after you go back out into the garden for your third (and final) load of pollen, you'll return to the hive with so much pollen that you won't even be able to talk. Your little bee cheeks will be so full, all you'll be able to do is just stand there and buzz. This is the signal to the queen bee that he should say, "Buzz, Buzz, Little Bee. Give it all to me." Have him practice that phrase as well.

When he has learned his line, go out for your third load of pollen—but when you do, go behind a wall or chair and get a mouthful of water. You return, and as instructed, the queen bee says "Buzz, Buzz, Little Bee. Give it all to me." At that point you spit your mouthful of water all over your queen bee.

Note: This stunt can also be done as a prearranged skit. Sometimes it's wise to clue your volunteer in ahead of time and make sure he doesn't say "Oh, no, you don't! I'm not going to get water spit all over me!" and spoil your skit. It should appear that your volunteer has "fallen for it," and it can be done that way without cluing him in if you choose a good sucker. Sometimes it's wiser to "fix it."

CHIKI-CHIKI

For this one, get four volunteers to come to the front of the room and line up facing the audience, side by side, with you at one end of the line. Tell the volunteers they must do exactly what you do because it is a coordination test to see (1) how well they can follow the leader, and (2) how well they can improvise on what he does. The audience will be the judge as to who does the best job.

Begin by swinging your arm in a circular, sweeping motion, and reach over and pinch the volunteer standing next to you on the cheek and say "Cheeky cheeky." Then that guy does the same to the next person in line, and so on. Next you wind up and grab the other cheek, and do the same. Then you pinch his nose in the same way, saying "Nosey nosey," and his chin while saying "chinnie, chinnie." With each of these, the same action is repeated down the line.

What makes this funny is that before your pinch the guy next to you each time, you put lipstick on your fingers with a tube that you have in your other hand, but concealed to the guy next to you. You just keep smearing lipstick all over the guy's face and the audience gets a lot of laughs, but the poor guy has no idea what they are laughing at.

Note: It's best to tell all the guys to stand with their hands behind their backs. That way you can keep the lipstick tube behind your back.

DONKEY

Have five or six volunteers come to the front of the room, then announce to the group that each volunteer will be secretly told the name of a barnyard animal. When you count to three, each of these people will try to make the sound of the animal that they were given as loudly as possible. The audience will judge who has done the best job. The winner will get a nice prize.

Then you whisper in the ear of each of the volunteers. But instead of giving them an animal, you tell all but one of them to not make a sound. That lucky one you tell to make a sound like a donkey. Of course, he thinks that all the others are going to imitate animals just like he does. Just before you count to three, remind them to make their noise as loudly as they can. The result will be a slightly embarrassed "donkey."

Don't forget to give him his prize.

ELEPHANT PANTOMIME

You'll need at least three volunteers for this one. Send them out of the room, tell the audience what's going to happen, and then call volunteer A back in.

Begin by telling volunteer A to watch you do a pantomime and to try and remember it as well as possible. Then, while he is watching, you pantomime "washing an elephant."

Only the audience knows what you are doing. The volunteers do not. After A watches you do the pantomime, B is brought into the room and A must do the pantomime for B, even though A may not know exactly what he is doing. He just tries to duplicate what you did. Then C is brought in and B does the pantomime (as close as he can get it) for C. The result is a lot of laughs, because the pantomime keeps getting farther and farther away from the original. Let the volunteers try to guess then what they were supposed to be pantomiming.

Here's how your original pantomime should go: Pull the elephant in on a rope. Tie the rope at a stake. Dip a rag in a pail and wash the side of the elephant, jumping high to get all the way to the top. Crawl underneath, wash his belly and legs. Go to the front and wash his trunk, inside and out, and wash the elephant's ears as well. Then wash under his tail, hold your nose, etc., and generally try to be as creative as possible.

FIRST KISS

Have several volunteers leave the room. Before you bring them back in, explain to the audience that when each person returns, the audience should be very quiet and not say a word. The M.C. (you) will also not say anything. Explain to the audience that what the volunteers say during that confused silence will be what they said right after their first kiss. As soon as the audience understands, bring the volunteers back in, one at a time. The confused volunteer, returning to nothing but silence, will undoubtedly say something. ("Now what do I do?" or "This is really weird," and so on.) Let each one talk (to the audience's delight) until he runs dry or gives up, and then bring in the next.

FIXED CHARADES

Two volunteers are sent out of the room with an assistant who explains to them that they are going to play a simple game of "charades." They each get a movie, book, or song title that they must get the audience to identify. Whoever does it in the fastest time wins.

   Meanwhile, you reveal to the audience (while the volunteers are out of the room) what the titles are that they will be "charad-ing." The first volunteer should have a difficult title, like "Mutiny on the Bounty." But the audience, already knowing what it is, should pretend to puzzle over it for a few seconds, then pick up quickly on the volunteer's clues and guess it after about ten seconds or so. The second volunteer will have a ridiculously easy one, like "Tea for Two." The audience should be very animated and make lots of guesses—all wrong. For example, if the person makes the letter "T" with his hands, the audience should guess "time out," or "hand signal," or anything but "tea." The result is a very frustrated volunteer.

FLY FAMILY

Send three or four volunteers out of the room. When they return (one at a time) tell them they are going to be introduced to the "Fly Family"—four people who stand in line with their hands behind their backs: Mr. Horsefly, Mrs. Horsefly, Mr. Butterfly, and finally Mr. Letterfly. They are introduced one at a time, shaking hands—but Letterfly throws a cup of water all over the unsuspecting fall guy.

THE FUNNEL TRICK

Have a volunteer (preferably a boy) come forward to try a little game, with a chance to win some money. Place a funnel in the boy's pants (in front). Have him tip his head back, and then place a quarter on his forehead. Tell him that if he can drop the quarter into the funnel three times in succession, he can keep the quarter. Chances are good he'll succeed the first two tries. On the third try, while his head is tipped back, grab a glass of water and pour it down the funnel.

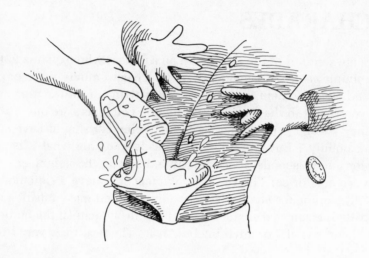

THE HOBBY QUIZ

Choose three guys in the room who have a hobby of some kind (any hobby). Explain to them that the audience is going to ask them questions about their hobby, and that they are to answer without giving away what their hobby actually is—this is because the audience is supposed to guess their hobbies. Then send them out of the room (supposedly so that the audience can think up some questions). While they are out, you tell the audience that they are to assume that all three boys' hobby is *kissing*. (Regardless of what their hobbies actually are.) Call the boys back in, and ask them questions like the ones below. Their answers will be hilarious.

1. Who taught you your hobby?
2. How long does it take to do your hobby?
3. In which room (or what place) do you perform your hobby?
4. What sound does your hobby make?
5. Is there any special training involved? If so, what?
6. How old were you when you first learned your hobby?
7. How do you get ready for your hobby?
8. What's the best time of the day to perform your hobby?

9. What do you wear when you are doing your hobby?
10. What sort of special equipment do you need?

MIND POWER

Rig up a box or a table draped with a cloth, big enough for a person to hide under. A balloon attached to a plastic tube or hose should be arranged so that only the balloon shows above the box, with the hose inserted through a hole in the box so that the person underneath may regulate the size of the balloon. Have a stool or chair next to the box with dummy electrical wires running into the box.

HE'S INVISIBLE TO AUDIENCE

Announce to the audience that this is a machine to measure a person's mental capacity—the smarter he is, the larger the balloon will become. Have several volunteers come up, one at a time, and lay their heads down on the seat of the stool; have the balloon increase in size a little more each time. Have the youth director come; the balloon shrinks. Finally say that you are tired and sit down on the seat—the balloon explodes.

ODDBALL

This is one of the funniest stunts of all time. It's best in a meeting format, when you have an audience and a stage or "up front" area. To begin, you select four or five contestants to compete in an exciting new game. They must leave the room (to a soundproof area) while you set up the game.

You'll need two or three tables that are the same width and about seven or eight balls of different kinds. Place the tables end-to-end and cover them with blankets to give the appearance of one long continuous table. But a hole has been cut in one of the blankets, and a person kneels or sits between two of the tables with his head sticking up through the hole. The balls are evenly spaced along the length of the table, with the head counting as one ball. All the balls (and the head) are then covered with towels so that they are completely covered. The crowd is warned not to reveal to the contestants what is going on.

Another—and even better—way to do this would be to actually cut a hole in the table top for the head to stick through. But that might not go over too well with whoever owns the table. If set up properly, the first method will work fine. When you're ready to go, there are several ways to play the game with your contestants:

1. *Name that Ball:* The announcer introduces the first volunteer and the crowd cheers wildly. The announcer explains that on the table are a number of different kinds of balls—volleyballs, footballs, soccerballs, and so on. The object of the game is for the contestant to start at one end of the table, tear off the first towel, and identify the kind of ball before proceeding to the next one. A timekeeper is clocking each contestant, and the winner will be the one who has the fastest time. The crowd is encouraged to cheer them on. When they tear off the towel covering the head, the head suddenly yells "BOO!" with his eyes bugging out. Nine out of ten contestants will jump right out of their socks. Have the contestants (rather than the head) face the audience, since their reaction is what makes this so hilarious.

2. *Guess that Ball:* Give the head a mouthful of water before each contestant comes in. You still use the "game show" motif but this time the contestant is guessing what is under each towel. The announcer tells the contestant at the start that he or she cannot touch the ball but must guess what each ball is before taking the towel off to see if they were correct. The contestant with the most correct guesses wins. If a correct guess is made, the crowd cheers; if wrong, they boo. It is important that the head stay perfectly still. When the contestant comes to the head, he guesses, then pulls off the towel. The head spits water all over the contestant.

3. *The Double-cross:* For both of the games above, a good way to end is to double-cross the head. He thinks he is so funny and is really enjoying spitting and scaring people. Let your last contestant know what's up ahead of time so that he goes through the motions all right, but when he uncovers the head, he gets him with water, pie, potatoes, mud, or something equally messy. It's really funny.

PINCHY-WINCHY

This stunt is set up as a game—boys against girls. Have three couples volunteer to compete, and have them come up front to play the game one couple at a time. First, the boy faces the girl, grabs her cheek with his thumb and forefinger, and says "pinchy-winchy" while making faces or whatever, trying to make her laugh. If the boy is successful, he gets one point, and if he is unsuccessful, the girl gets one point. Then the girl gets to pinch the boy's cheek, saying "pinchy-winchy" and making a face or whatever she wants to try and make the boy laugh. After three tries on each side, the next couple plays, and then the last couple.

By now, the last couple is really going to give it all they've got and try to score big. At least that's what the boy thinks. The girl has armed herself, without the boy's knowledge, with a tube of lipstick which she holds behind her back. Every time she pinches the boy's cheek, she puts a little lipstick on her fingers first and rubs the lipstick on his face. The boy doesn't realize what's going on till it's too late, allowing his face to literally be painted. The audience loves it.

PLATE HYPNOTISM

Explain to the audience that you have had some experience in college with hypnotism. You learned a relatively obscure method of hypnotism called "plate hypnotism." Ask if there is anyone in the group who would like to be hypnotized. Usually you will get someone to volunteer, since most of the kids don't really believe you can do it anyway. Make sure your volunteer is someone who doesn't wear glasses.

Ask your volunteer to sit down. Give him (or her) a plate to hold in his hand. (It must be a ceramic or china plate.) He must hold it by the edge with his left hand, perfectly level so that the "magic power" won't spill out of the plate. Then you sit across from him, facing him, about 10 feet away. You also have a plate. Your volunteer is instructed to stare directly into your eyes, and do everything that you do, except talking. You also ask the audience to be as quiet as possible. You then begin by taking your finger (right hand) and rubbing the top of the plate, then rubbing it between your eyes. Do this over and over while saying something like, "We're getting the hypnotic power from the top of the plate and rubbing it into the eyes. You are getting sleepier and sleepier." After a few moments of this, you move to the edges of the plate with your finger, then finally you rub the bottom of the plate. The volunteer should be doing the same. You continue to chatter: "Now we are getting hypnotic power from the bottom of the plate and rubbing it around our eyes. Your eyes are getting heavier and sleepier." This is where the fun begins. Beforehand, you charred the bottom of the volunteer's plate with a match, so that as he rubs the bottom of the plate, and then his eyes, he is smearing black soot all over his face. He is not aware of this, of course, because he is staring you straight in the eyes and can't see his finger. Continue until he catches on, then show him a mirror.

PSYCHOLOGICAL STORY

Send three volunteers out of the room, then explain to the rest of the group that you are going to tell the volunteers a story, one at a time. The story is symbolic, and only the audience is clued in as to what the symbols in the story mean:

1. The forest. It represents life. In other words, if a person sees his forest as dark and gloomy, then that would be his outlook on life.
2. The key. It represents education.
3. The cup. It represents religion.
4. The water. It represents sex.
5. The bear. It represents life's problems.
6. The wall. It represents death.

Then bring the volunteers back into the room, one at a time, and tell them the following story. Explain to each that they are to use their imagination and be as creative and as descriptive as possible as they follow your instructions. The story should go something like this:

Imagine that you are in a forest. What does your imaginary forest look like? (Wait for the response.) You begin walking down a trail in the forest and find a key lying in the trail. Describe the key and tell us what you decide to do with it. (Response.) You go a little farther down the trail and you find a cup. Describe the cup and tell us what you do with it. (Response.) You continue down the trail and suddenly you reach some water. What does the water look like, and what is your response to it? (Response.) A short while later you find a bear. Describe the bear, what it does, and what you do. (Response.) Last of all you encounter a wall. Describe the wall and what you do on finding the wall. What is on the other side of the wall? (Response.)

After each volunteer has been told the story and responded, let them in on the meaning of the symbols. It is also wise to explain that this was done only for fun, and there is really no significance to either the symbolism or the volunteers' responses. This crowd-breaker is good for a lot of laughs, and works best with high-school students or older.

THE RUNNING SAP

Explain that you are an artist in your spare time and that you are going to paint a "human painting" right before the audience's eyes—using people instead of paint. The scene is in the forest. Have someone come up and be the "babbling brook" by standing up front going "babble babble babble . . ." over and over. Next have someone come up and be the rustling trees. He stands next to the babbling brook and goes "rustle rustle rustle . . ." Do the same thing with the "whistling grass" and the "howling wind," and then ask for someone to come up and be the picture frame. The frame runs continually around the other guys who are babbling, rustling, whistling, and howling. While they are all doing their part, you say, "And now, ladies and gentlemen, there you have it. The babbling brook, the rustling trees, the whistling grass, the howling wind, and the RUNNING SAP!"

SKYDIVING LESSON

This one works best in a room with soft carpet.

Three volunteers are chosen to learn how to skydive. One at a time, each volunteer is brought into the room and asked to stand on a sturdy 2 x 4 plank, which is lifted up by two strong boys. The volunteer uses the leader's shoulders as a brace, so he won't fall. The board is lifted up about three feet, then the contestant is asked to jump into a small circle for five points. The board is lifted higher, and he jumps again for ten points. The last time, for twenty points, he must jump blindfolded. But this time, the strong boys lift the board only two or three inches, and the leader stoops down real low, giving the blindfolded contestant the feeling that he is high. He jumps, but usually falls flat on his face.

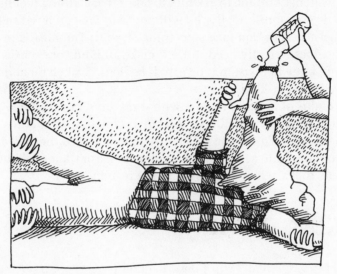

SUBMARINE RIDE

A volunteer lies flat on his back on a table with a person at each arm and each leg. The legs are the left and right rudders. The arms are torpedo one and torpedo two. A jacket is put over the volunteer's head with one sleeve directly over his nose. This is the periscope. The captain (you) yells "Left rudder!" (Person on left leg raises leg.) "Right rudder!" (Raise right leg.) "Torpedo one!" "Torpedo two!" (Raise arms.) "Up periscope!" (Sleeve is lifted straight up.) "Dive! Dive!" (You pour water down sleeve and into the volunteer's face.)

TAKE OFF WHAT YOU DON'T NEED

Have a guy come up, lie down on a table, and cover him with a blanket. Tell him to take off something that he doesn't need, and toss it off the table. He will usually take off something like his shoes, or a wristwatch. Continue to ask him to take off something that he doesn't need, and he will continue to do so—until, finally, he will refuse to take off anything else. But don't let him off so easy—insist that he *can* take something else off. The idea is to get him to take off the *blanket*, since he doesn't really need it. He'll make all kinds of excuses as to why he can't take anything else off, but you insist that he can. If he doesn't catch on and has to be told, give him a silly penalty of some kind.

A good variation of this old trick is to do it with three guys, bringing them into the room one at a time to go through the same gag. But the last guy is clued in—under his pants he's wearing a pair of swimming trunks. To the amazement of the audience, he will take off everything (except for the swimming trunks, which the audience doesn't know about). Then he throws the blanket off—and that's when the girls start screaming.

THE TALKING HEAD

This is a variation of the "Oddball" stunt described on page 174. To set it up, use a table that extends in the center, or place two card tables ten or twelve inches apart and drape with sheets to the floor. Cut a hole in the sheet big enough for a guy's head to come through. Place three buckets upside down on top of the table, one of them over the hole. During a busy part of your meeting (or behind a curtain), have the guy acting as the "talking head" position himself under the table with his head sticking up through the sheet and under a bucket. No one in the group should be able to tell that there is anyone under the table.

Ask three volunteers (preferably girls) to leave the room, and bring them back in one at a time. Explain that they are helping with the Evelyn Wood Speed Reading Course and have only two seconds to read the short printed phrase under bucket #1, only four seconds for bucket #2, and only six seconds for bucket #3. When they are ready, position them with their faces close to the bucket's edge, lifting the bucket just long enough for them to see and read the phrase. Lower the bucket and have them tell the group what they read. Repeat for the second bucket amid much praise and encouragement for the fine job they are doing. When they are positioned and ready for the third bucket, lift it much higher and your talking head should scream or yell to scare the volunteer. This first time, even the group will scream and react since they were not expecting to see a head under the bucket. Repeat the process for the second victim, making sure that the group has been cued not to give anything away.

"THERE'S A B'AR!"

Get several volunteers (kids) to line up in a straight line, facing the audience, shoulder to shoulder, with the leader at the right-hand end of the line (*his* right, not the audience's). The leader says, "There's a b'ar!" (*bear*); the kids are instructed to say, "War?" (*where*). The leader responds with, "Thar!" and points to a spot off to his left but with his *right* arm. The kids are instructed to point also, and keep pointing. Again the leader says "There's a b'ar!" The kids reply, "War?" and the leader says, "Thar!" and this time points to his right with his *left* arm. The kids do the same and now have both arms pointing (crisscrossed). The same steps are repeated, this time with the leader squatting and pointing with his left leg to the right. All the kids do the same. Once more the same is repeated and the kids must point with their *noses* to the left. So now the kids' faces are turned to the left, away from the leader—who then gives the guy next to him a push, and the entire line will fall like dominoes.

THE TRAINED FLEA ACT

One person is introduced to the group as having a very unusual hobby—flea-training. He has agreed to bring his best flea and give a demonstration to the group. The flea-trainer goes to the front of the group and begins his pleasant but serious presentation. He introduces his most talented and highly skilled flea by name, such as Myrtle. He explains how many months he has worked with her and how hard it is to bring a flea to her level of performance. The patter can include an explanation of the varying personalities of fleas and their individual capacities. He may have her in a little box or jar. As he takes her out, he mentions that with good eyesight and some practice, one can recognize fleas by their manners and markings.

Then the act begins. He carefully releases her from his hand and follows her imaginary slow circular flight in the air, speaking soft words of encouragement. After her return, he releases her for a double flight—with some anxiety, because she has never performed in front of a group before—but she makes it. Next, she is to attempt three circles. But on the third her flight becomes wobbly and erratic as he follows with his eyes and forefinger. She veers out into the audience; he calls her with alarm and plunges after her, never taking his eyes off her.

He follows her to some member of the audience who makes a good butt for a joke, such as a leader or extrovert. Quickly, he extricates her from the fellow's hair down the back of his neck. Greatly relieved, he takes her back toward the front of the stage, speaking softly to her in his cupped hand—then spins back toward the audience in alarm and yells with dismay, "Hey—you're not Myrtle!"

THE UGLIEST MONSTER IN THE WORLD

Bring in a guy with a blanket over his head who is the "monster." Tell everybody that this monster is so ugly that anyone who looks at him falls over dead. Three guys in the audience (clued-in) come up to try. They look under the blanket and, sure enough, they scream and fall over dead. Now choose a girl (unsuspecting) to come up and look under the blanket, just to prove that girls are the stronger sex. She comes up, looks under the blanket, and when she does . . . the monster screams and falls dead.

CHAPTER SIX

AUDIENCE PARTICIPATION

THE ANTIQUE SHOP

This skit calls for a bare stage, since the individuals called from the audience are to be the props and scenery. You'll need seven volunteers. They can be a mixed selection, but it's best to have at least three boys to act as two chairs and a table. The other props—potted plant, window, door, and lamp—can be handled by girls. You'll need just a few additional props: a sprinkling can, a flashlight, and some dishes.

Send one member of the cast out to explain that the local furniture shop who had agreed to provide the props didn't come through, and that unless you can get seven volunteers to help out, you won't be able to perform the wonderful play you've prepared. Explain that the volunteers won't be harmed and that they'll be in a great spot to see the show.

When you have your volunteers, have one fellow get down on hands and knees in the center of the stage and explain that he's a table. Another volunteer becomes a lamp—have her stand with one arm extended, holding the flashlight (turned off). Two more fellows are chairs, one on either side of the table on hands and knees. The other volunteers are a potted plant, a window—which should be near the potted plant—and a door, which is positioned right where the actors will enter. Show the door how to hold one arm out for the actors to enter through, and how to move the arm when the actors push through. Remind your props not to smile or make any sound, and you're ready to begin.

Hilda: (*Entering through the door. She moves the door's arm and swings it back into place.*) Oh, I thought there was someone in here. But there isn't. Just a room full of antiques.

Tom: (*entering*) Hello.

Hilda: Hello.

Tom: Don't I know you?

Hilda: You should. I'm Hilda, the girl you had a date with today.

Tom: I don't believe it.

Hilda: It's true. And you're Tom.

Tom: Yes. Isn't it strange that we should make a date in such an odd-looking room?

Hilda: It is odd. But what can you expect in a store that sells nothing but antiques?

Tom: Are you interested in antiques?

Hilda:	Very much.
Tom:	Have you noticed the lamp over here?
Hilda:	It caught my eye immediately. What a monstrosity!
Tom:	It's one of the first electric lamps to be made—by Thomas Edison.
Hilda:	Let's see if it works.
Jim:	*(entering)* What's going on here?
Tom:	Oh, hello, Jim. Hilda, this is Jim. He owns the store. That's why I wanted to meet you here. I knew he could show us around the place.
Hilda:	Hello, Jim.
Jim:	Hello, Hilda. Yes, I'll be glad to show you anything.
Hilda:	I was amazed at the styles of some of these antiques. We were just discussing this lamp.
Jim:	That's a very old and rare antique. Notice the lines and the engraving on the upper part. *(indicates the lamp's face)*
Hilda:	It looks like it has weathered many storms.
Jim:	It has. I think she was discarded by several buyers before she finally landed in here.
Tom:	Will it burn?
Jim:	Oh, yes. It burns all right. *(He turns on the flashlight in the hand of the lamp.)*
Tom:	Now it looks more grotesque than ever.
Hilda:	Yes, some of its ugly features were hidden before, but now it shows up all the lines. UGH, I wouldn't want that around my house.
Jim:	*(turning away)* Well, we antique dealers can't be too choosy. Sometimes we must handle things we don't want.
Tom:	What about this flower pot?
Hilda:	That, too, is odd.
Jim:	This pot dates back one hundred years.
Tom:	It looks older than that.
Hilda:	And it has a flower in it. How old is that?
Jim:	I just planted that about a month ago. I did it to add a little appeal to the flower pot.
Hilda:	It looks wilted.
Jim:	I just noticed that. I'll bet Sara forgot to water that plant again. Oh, Sara!
Sara:	*(offstage)* Yes, sir?
Jim:	Have you forgotten to water the plant again?

Sara:	Yes, sir, I did forget.
Jim:	You'd better do it right now.
Sara:	Yes, sir, I'll do it right now. *(She enters with the sprinkling can. Whether it has water in it is left to the judgment of the characters.)*
Jim:	That plant will wilt entirely if you don't water it, Sara.
Sara:	I'm sorry, sir, it won't happen again. I just forgot. But I'll give it a good drink right now. *(She holds the sprinkling can over the potted plant.)*
Jim:	That will do, Sara.
Sara:	Yes, sir. But I'm afraid ordinary water won't do much good in this case.
Jim:	We'll see, Sara, we'll see. *(Sara exits.)* And now what can I show you folks?
Tom:	I like that table.
Jim:	It isn't bad, but it isn't on the level.
Hilda:	Not on the level?
Jim:	No, it's old and crooked. Let me show you. *(He puts a few of the dishes on it.)* See. They don't sit well.
Tom:	It isn't too bad.
Jim:	Now watch. I'll put this pitcher of water right in the center and you'll see what happens. *(He does.)* See, the pitcher is liable to spill. The thing is crooked.
Hilda:	You'd never think it to look at it.
Jim:	*(leaving the pitcher on the table)* How about these chairs?
Tom:	I noticed them.
Jim:	Now these are real antiques.
Hilda:	How old are they?
Jim:	They date back to pre-Civil War days.
Hilda:	Think of that!
Tom:	Are they strong?
Jim:	Try one.
Tom:	Thanks, I think I will. *(He sits on a chair.)*
Hilda:	*(There's a horn offstage.)* That's for me. I'll just look out the window and see if I'm right. *(She goes to the window.)* This is an awfully dirty window, Jim.
Jim:	Yes, I can't do much with it.
Hilda:	I can hardly see through it. *(Looks.)* No, I guess that wasn't for me after all.
Jim:	I'm sorry about the window, Hilda. It just seems to gather dirt from everywhere.

Tom:	(sitting on one of the chairs) You ought to try this chair, Hilda. It's really comfortable.
Hilda:	You wouldn't think so to look at it.
Jim:	No, it's kind of bony looking, but it'll fool you.
Tom:	Try it with me. (He moves over on the man's back.)
Hilda:	(She sits with Tom.) Say, I had no idea that it was this comfortable.
Tom:	I think I hear it creaking. Maybe we're too heavy for it. (Ad lib until the chair breaks down.)
Hilda:	Oh, dear me, Tom, we broke the chair.
Tom:	I'm so sorry, Jim.
Jim:	Think nothing of it. After all, it was kind of old and decrepit and it didn't take much to break it down.
Hilda:	I really feel badly about this.
Jim:	I don't want you to feel that way. Just to prove that there is nothing to worry about, I want you to sit on the other chair.
Tom:	But suppose it should break down?
Jim:	It won't. Sit on it.
Tom:	Well, if you insist. (as he sits on the other chair)
Jim:	You too, Hilda. Try it.
Hilda:	I don't think I should.
Jim:	Please do.
Hilda:	All right, if you say so. (She sits on the chair with Tom.)
Jim:	There! Isn't that a much better chair?
Hilda:	Yes, much better. It seems more solid.
Tom:	Yes, especially up here in front. (touching the man's head)
Hilda:	We had a chair something like this at one time.
Jim:	Did you?
Hilda:	Yes, then one day it broke. I felt so sorry about that. (And so they continue to ad lib until the other chair breaks down.)
Hilda:	Oh, we've done it again.
Tom:	I knew we shouldn't have sat on that antique.
Jim:	Now, now, there's nothing to worry about.
Hilda:	But I insisted that you sit on it. It's my fault.
Tom:	Well, if that's the way you feel about it. But we must go now, Jim.

Hilda: Yes, we really must go. Thanks for bothering with us, Jim.
Jim: It was a pleasure.
Tom: I'll see you later.
Jim: Let me walk to your car with you. Right out this door.

BEAUTIFUL BESSIE

For this skit, either divide your group into ten small groups or have ten individuals come to the front and make the sound effects described below. The narrator reads the script, and whenever he gets to one of the names listed below, the person or group assigned that name yells out the proper sound effect.

Characters:

Rattlesnakes—hiss rattle rattle, hiss rattle rattle
Cowboys—yippee
Bessie—screams (should be a boy)
Love—loud kissing sound
Bandits—Grr-r-r-r
Horses—stamp feet
Cattle—moo-o-o-o-o
Guns—bang, bang
Wolves—yow-o-o-o-o
Villain—(gruffly) Hah-h-h-h-h-h-h-h-Hah-h-h-h-Hah-h-h-h-h-h

At the end of the story, when reader says, "Ride 'em, cowboy!" all jump to their feet and yell their part in mass.

The Story:

There once was a handsome cowboy . . . named Bill Jones, who lived far, far out West on a great ranch. He spent most of his days riding the range on a fine black horse . . . named Napoleon, and following his herds of bawling white-faced cattle . . .

On an adjoining ranch lived beautiful Bessie . . . Brown with her aged parents. All the cowboys . . . loved . . . Bessie . . . but especially did the heart of the handsome Bill go pitter-patter when he looked into her eyes which were limpid pools of darkness. The bold bandit . . . Two Gun . . . Sam also did feign to win the heart of beautiful Bessie . . . but she spurned his love . . .

One day Bessie's father and mother received a letter asking them to come to town at once, because the ruthless villain . . . was about to foreclose on the mortgage to their ranch. Mr. Brown hitched up their horses, . . . they put their guns . . . in the wagon, Mrs. Brown placed her rattlesnake . . . charm in her purse, and they drove away to town.

"Ahh-Hah," cried the bold bandit . . . Two Gun . . . Sam, when they were out of sight; for he had forged the letter. "Now, I shall have the love . . . of the Beautiful Bessie" . . . So he rode his horse . . . up to the house and shot both of his guns . . . Beautiful Bessie . . . ran out of the house to see if someone had killed a wolf . . . or a rattlesnake . . ."

When the girl saw Two Gun . . . Sam, she started to run for her horse . . . But the bold bandit . . . grabbed her by the wrist. "Ah, proud beauty," said he. "You shall be my wife, and someday I shall own all of your father's cattle . . ."

"Never," said Bessie . . . "I do not love . . . you."

"Then perhaps, you would rather be taken to a den of rattlesnakes . . . or eaten by the wolves . . . or trampled by the cattle . . .

"Yes! Yes! Anything rather than let you steal my love . . . and take my father's cattle . . . Unhand me, you villain . . ."

"Very well, proud beauty, to the rattlesnakes . . . we go." And he put her on a horse . . . and sped away.

Gun . . . shots rang out, and two bullets went through the top of the bold bandit's . . . sombrero. "Stop, villain! . . . Rattlesnake! . . . Wolf! . . ." It was the handsome cowboy . . . Bill Jones.

When Two Gun . . . Sam saw the cowboy . . . he muttered to himself, "Coises, foiled again." He dropped beautiful Bessie . . . from his horse . . . threw his gun . . . away and started for the hills where the wolves . . . the rattlesnakes . . . and cattle . . . roam, for he knew he would never win the love . . . of Bessie . . . nor get her father's cattle . . .

The handsome cowboy . . . looked into the eyes of the beautiful Bessie . . . which were still limpid pools of darkness, and they both forgot about the wolves . . . and the rattlesnakes . . . and the villain . . . who wanted Mr. Brown's cattle . . .

Bessie . . . thanked the handsome cowboy . . . for rescuing her from the bold bandit . . . and told Bill that she had been saving her love . . . for him. So they rode off together on their horses . . . *Ride 'em, cowboy!*

CHANNEL CHANGERS

The following three scripts all follow the same format. The idea is to demonstrate what might happen if you flipped back and forth between several different programs or channels on your radio or television set.

These skits can be rehearsed, or they can be done in an impromptu fashion by selecting volunteers to read each part in front of the group. Each person will need a script. For added effect, give each speaker an appropriate hat, costume, or prop to help identify the role that they are portraying.

Each "click" in the script is a channel change. Use your own creativity, add your own lines, and have fun with these.

Script #1: Television

Story Lady:	Today, boys and girls, our story is about Little Red Riding Hood. Once upon a time there was a little girl named Little Red Riding Hood. One day her mother asked her to go through the woods to visit her grandmother. And on her way who should jump out from behind a tree but . . . *(click)*
Boy Scout:	The Boy Scouts of America! Yes, sir, fellas, the Boy Scouts are just the group for you. Why, for just a dollar . . . *(click)*
Gangster:	You can shove it down your throat! Try and steal my gal, will ya? Why for two cents I'd . . . *(click)*
Recipe Lady:	. . . set carefully in a quart of prune juice. And when the mixture is settled, ladies, just pop it into the . . . *(click)*
Announcer:	. . . end zone for a touchdown! Wow! Did you see that last play, sports fans? Terrific! And now a word from our sponsor, Shavo. With Shavo, the sharpest razor in the world . . . *(click)*

Gangster:	You can cut your own throat for all I care, you slob! Who do you think you are anyway? . . . *(click)*
Story Lady:	. . . Little Red Riding Hood . . . *(click)*
Recipe Lady:	What a smell! Doesn't that just make your mouth water, ladies? Now for the vegetables. Ladies, this next recipe is very unique. It calls for one . . . *(click)*
Announcer:	. . . broken leg! The star is definitely out of the game. The wildcats really need help. Guess they'll have to call in the . . . *(click)*
Boy Scout:	. . . Boy Scouts of America! Each year, fellas, we take a camping trip. Boy, there's nothing like it. You're out there all alone with no one but the wind, the stars, and . . . *(click)*
Story Lady:	. . . Little Red Riding Hood. As she entered the cottage she said . . . *(click)*
Gangster:	This is the dumbest thing I've ever done! How could I have ever called you a friend when you turn on me and steal my girl. You slob! You're nothing but a . . . *(click)*
Recipe Lady:	. . . hot dog! Slice it carefully and then cook the casserole on top of the . . . *(click)*
Announcer:	. . . football field. That should do it for the Wildcats, folks. With Brooks out of the game, it doesn't look like they have a chance. Now they line up. The snap. Draw play! What a hand-off. There goes Johnson! Look at him go. He's going all the way to the . . . *(click)*
Boy Scout:	. . . outhouse. We don't have running water either. You'll learn how to make Mulligan stew, though. You'd be surprised how it tastes in the fresh air and woods. After a hearty meal, you can't help but say . . . *(click)*
Gangster:	I think I'll shoot myself! That gal meant more to me than . . . *(click)*
Recipe Lady:	. . . a handful of chopped nuts. Chop them fine and fold into the flour mixture. Next, beat the eggs until they look like . . . *(click)*
Announcer:	. . . mud in your face. What a pile up! The Panthers didn't even get past the line of scrimmage! Boy, these Wildcats have really worked hard this half. With the score at 10–10 and five minutes to go, who will win? . . . *(click)*
Boy Scout:	The Boy Scouts of America! Boy, fellas, you can't pass up this opportunity to join now. Right now you're probably saying to yourself . . . *(click)*
Story Lady:	What a big mouth you have! And the wolf said . . . *(click)*

Gangster:	Listen, honey. You're comin' with me. I'm tired of all this foolin' around. And you, ya dirty yellow rat, you're nothin' but a . . . *(click)*
Announcer:	. . . hound dog running down the field! Oh-oh. It looks like he's heading right for the . . . *(click)*
Recipe Lady:	. . . garbage. There's no need to keep it. After this dinner, ladies, you'll sigh with satisfaction. Your husband will tell you it's delicious and you'll say, "Oh, you . . . *(click)*

Script #2: Radio

Person A:	Good evening, ladies and gentlemen. This is Seymour Skidmarks bringing you the latest news in the world of sports. The annual football game between _____ and _____ was played last week to the enjoyment of a large crowd who went wild when, at a crucial point in the game, Coach _____ sent in . . . *(click)*
Person B:	. . . three eggs, a cup of buttermilk, and a pinch of salt. Stir well and pour into a flat greased pan or . . . *(click)*
Person C:	. . . your new fall hat. This year, fashion decrees that women shall wear a large variety of charm bracelets. A most popular design is to make them of . . . *(click)*
Person D:	. . . old whiskers? If you do, just shave them off with Bates' Better Shaving Cream. Use this cream, and you will be so handsome that all the girls will . . . *(click)*
Person E:	. . . bend over and touch the floor twenty times. This exercise is superb for general reducing. All right now, pupils, again let's bend over, up, over . . . *(click)*
Person F:	*(singing)* . . . the ocean. My Bonnie lies over the sea. My Bonnie lies over the ocean, oh, bring back my Bonnie . . . *(click)*
Person A:	. . . _____ who sailed down the field for a touchdown that tied the game. What a play! What a perfect . . . *(click)*
Person C:	. . . ly darling little summer bag that all you girls simply must have. At first glimpse they may remind one of . . . *(click)*
Person G:	. . . a bowl of porridge. But it was toooo hot. The second bowl was as hot as the first, but the third was just right. Goldilocks ate, and ate, until she could . . . *(click)*

Person D: . . . feel the stiff beard with your hand. Is that very romantic? Our foolproof way to get a girl friend is to . . . *(click)*

Person E: . . . breathe deeply three times, and pound on your chest with your fists after inhaling each breath. This enlivens the tissues and makes one feel . . . *(click)*

Person B: . . . puffy and full of air. You achieve this effect by beating the mixture with a rotary eggbeater for five . . . *(click)*

Person C: . . . hundred years. The things our grandmothers wore then are the most popular things today. Already fashion leaders, prominent society women are trying to bring back more old-fashioned manners. Their cry is "Bring back . . . *(click)*

Person F: . . . *(singing)* my Bonnie to me, to me, bring back, bring back, oh, bring back . . . *(click)*

Person D: . . . a nice soft chin and a host of compliments. If you use our cream, those whiskers will come out with a . . . *(click)*

Person G: CRASH!! Goldilocks had broken the little chair all to pieces. Then she jumped up and started up the stairs. There she saw three beds. The first bed was covered with a bearskin rug, which was too soft. The second bed was covered with . . . *(click)*

Person A: . . . what looked like crawling things from the press box, but it was only the players in hard scrimmage. We are looking with expectation to _____ winning their _____ championship this fall. The players are in good condition; their average weight is . . . *(click)*

Person E: . . . 110 pounds. You, too, can weigh this much if you just follow these simple exercises. Don't take them too hard at first or you will probably have to . . . *(click)*

Person F: . . . *(singing)* lay on my pillow. Last night as I lay on my bed; last night as I lay on my pillow, I dreamed that my Bonnie was . . . *(click)*

Person B: . . . cooking in a hot oven at about 450 degrees Fahrenheit. For an extra treat, garnish with cloves or whole. . . *(click)*

Person G: . . . bears? Will Goldilocks get home safely? How will the story end? Keep your radio tuned to this station until tomorrow at this time for the next episode of this thrilling story. Until then, kiddies, be sweet and don't forget to . . . *(click)*

Person D: . . . shave off the whiskers with Bates'. Our motto is . . . *(click)*

Person E: . . . stand on your head and wave your feet in the air. Gym clothes are best for this exercise, but . . . *(click)*

Person C:	. . . an ostrich feather will do just as well. Take my tip and you girls will be as fashionable as . . . (click)
Person A:	. . . _____, from whom we are expecting great things this year. This is your friendly announcer, Seymour Skidmarks, signing off and saying . . . (click)
Person C:	. . . Night all! (sexy voice)

Script #3: Television

Indy 500:	Here we are at the Indy 500 and we're almost ready to begin. GENTLEMEN . . . START YOUR . . . (click)
Health Advisor:	. . . toothbrushes. These are very important to our overall health. Every married couple ought to own and use . . . (click)
Gangster:	. . . handcuffs! There's no way I'll wear those things. It looks like I'm going to have to call . . . (click)
Sesame Street:	Big Bird! Come back! When it rains like this we all wear . . . (click)
Grocer:	. . . seedless grapefruits and oranges. Many people have a lot of trouble with seeds. Just imagine swallowing . . . (click)
Indy:	. . . an oil spill in the third turn! Unser is going to slide through. It looks like he's going to collide with . . . (click)
Sesame Street:	Cookie Monster! Where have you been? Boys and girls, we're going to take you to . . . (click)
Gangster:	. . . the county jail! I've got to get out of this joint! I hear the bank is expecting two million . . . (click)
Health:	. . . push-ups, sit-ups, and many other exercises. Remember, always breathe deeply before . . . (click)
Grocer:	. . . peeling a banana. You know, the aroma of a well-ripened banana is much like that of . . . (click)
Indy:	. . . gasoline all over the pit area! Now, there is the danger of fire! Rivera has jumped out of his . . . (click)
Sesame Street:	. . . garbage can. Children, the Cookie Monster has always wanted to . . . (click)
Gangster:	. . . rob the First National Bank! I think I can do it. The police would never think to look for me in the . . . (click)

Grocer:	. . . frozen food section. One thing I require here at Food King is that every check-out clerk should always . . . *(click)*
Indy:	. . . flip end over end. I've never seen such a crash. I believe the medical crew has a large number of . . . *(click)*
Health:	. . . jump ropes for all the children. These young bodies are . . . *(click)*
Sesame Street:	. . . yellow, green, purple, and orange. It is so beautiful. We must remember that rainbows . . . *(click)*
Gangster:	. . . are to be memorized and swallowed. These are confidential. Don't let anyone know . . . *(click)*
Grocer:	We sell live lobsters. We are very organized and reasonable. People go through our check-out lines . . . *(click)*
Indy:	. . . moving at over 200 miles per hour. Wow! What a car. Ladies and gentlemen, he is flying around . . . *(click)*
Health:	. . . your left kneecap. This can become a problem. Sometimes this won't develop until you . . . *(click)*
Sesame Street:	. . . let Big Bird give you a big hug! Oh, isn't that sweet! Big Bird loves to . . . *(click)*
Gangster:	. . . drive his car over a cliff. That's a 200-foot drop. He'll never live through . . . *(click)*
Grocer:	. . . our famous barbecued chicken. We've had some great customers. One man was rolling his cart down aisle three, and . . . *(click)*
Indy:	He blew a tire! He's spilling oil all over the track. Tell the clean-up crew to . . . *(click)*
Health:	Drink it all up! It's great for hair, bones, skin, and . . . *(click)*
Sesame Street:	. . . counting by twos. It's really not that hard. We've found that many children out there are . . . *(click)*
Gangster:	. . . holding my wife for ransom. Those lousy rats! I wouldn't give them . . . *(click)*
Grocer:	. . . rotten eggs! You won't find them here. Our eggs are the finest you'll find in any . . . *(click)*
Indy:	. . . gas tank! It looks like a bad leak. Yes, the gas is going all over his . . . *(click)*

Health:	Leotards. They are so comfortable, I wouldn't exercise without them. You might also buy . . . *(click)*
Sesame Street:	. . . huge shoes for those webbed feet. It's not often we have a duck on our . . . *(click)*
Gangster:	. . . pizza! Yeah, I got to eat and run. Charlie, don't forget to line up the . . . *(click)*
Grocer:	. . . tomatoes in a perfect row. In our meat section yesterday, we caught a man eating a . . . *(click)*
Indy:	. . . checkered flag! And that's all, folks!

CREATIVE THEME SKITS

Here's an impromptu skit idea for retreats or youth meetings that is creative and involves total participation. Divide your group into teams, and have a sack for each team—sacks you stuffed beforehand with ordinary objects like: paper clips, Q-tips, Popsicle sticks, and so on. Put the *same* things in each sack. Give each team twenty minutes to make up and rehearse a skit on a selected theme. The skit can be serious or funny, but each team must use every item in the sack and every team member must be involved. After the time limit, have each team present their skit.

THE LAND HAG

This audience-participation skit is particularly useful for a Halloween event, but can be used on any occasion when a bit of silliness is needed. Names of streets, places, and events may be changed to fit your crowd.

To begin, divide into five groups and assign each group a "key word" that has a corresponding action or sound. When they hear the key word in the story, they make the sound or action as instructed.

Andy Ambiguous—shrug shoulders and say "huhhh?"
Count Viscosity—with accent say, "I vant to drink your oil."

Sally—"Ahhhhhhhh" (sweetly)
Land Hag—a witch's evil cackle
Storm—thunder, wind, rumblings

Practice with the group first so that they have their parts down, then read the following story aloud, pausing briefly in the appropriate spaces so that the kids can add the sound effects.

The Land Hag

Once upon a time, long, long, ago and in the far away village of Beverly Hills, lived a beautiful and delicate maiden known simply as Sally (ahh). Now Sally (ahh) was a tender lass, who wore gingham and calico, ate apple pie, saluted the flag, watched "The Bob Newhart Show," and never gave anyone any trouble.

But alas, Sally (ahh) had a mean, cruel, ugly, nasty, horrible, crummy witch of a stepmother known throughout the area as the Land Hag (cackle). She spent her time casting spells, running up the inflation rate, and turning innocent little children into Pac-man machines.

Now the Land Hag (cackle) had a regular thing going with Count Viscosity (oil), a vampire who drank 10-40 when he couldn't get hold of any fresh blood. Count Viscosity (oil) lived in a coffin underneath the music building of the local college and had been terrorizing gas stations on Hollywood Boulevard. This was one reason for the recent energy crisis.

As it happens, Count Viscosity (oil) had just been stringing along the Land Hag (cackle) in hopes of actually marrying Sally (ahh) and inheriting Sally's (ahh) fortune, tied up in a Texas oil well which the Land Hag (cackle) controlled.

Now also as it happens, Sally (ahh), the Land Hag (cackle), and Count Viscosity (oil) were all afraid of storms (boom). The Land Hag (cackle) had once been struck by lightning during a storm (boom) while playing nine holes at a Malibu Country Club. Count Viscosity (oil) once slipped on an oily patch on the street during a storm (boom), and Sally (ahh) had sat through a rain-drenched Rose Parade. No wonder they feared storms (boom).

There is one other character in our story and that is our macho hero, Andy Ambiguous (huh). Andy (huh) never ate quiche, wore pink, or listened to Henry Mancini. Of course, Andy (huh) was in love with Sally (ahh) and thought that Count Viscosity (oil) was a wimp. But for all his macho ways, Andy (huh) was also afraid of storms (boom). One night while Andy (huh) was riding in his jeep, along came a storm (boom) and his cowboy hat shrank over his eyes. As

Andy (huh) *was stumbling around trying to get it off, he bungled into a theater showing* "Herbie Goes to the Chocolate Factory." *He was humiliated.*

(Get dramatic.)

The plot thickens. It was Halloween night, and there was an eerie feel in the air. As the sun went down, Count Viscosity (oil) came out from under the music building and took a bus toward Beverly Hills.

Just at that moment, Andy (huh) jumped in his jeep and also headed out to see his Sally (ahh). The Land Hag (cackle) was beginning to feel strange and was turning poor trick-or-treaters into a complete Atari video system.

As Andy (huh) and Count Viscosity (oil) drew closer, a storm (boom) broke out. Count Viscosity (oil) decided this was the night to ditch the Land Hag (cackle), marry Sally (ahh), do away with Andy (huh), and get the oil well.

Suddenly, there was an earthquake—then the dam broke, a hurricane blew in, inflation hit 15%, and oil went up to $200 a barrel.

At that moment, both Andy (huh) and Count Viscosity (oil) hit the door of the Land Hag (cackle).

The Count (oil) shouted, "Hag, (cackle), we're through. I'm a-marryin' Sally" (ahhh).

"Why, you oil-suckin' varmint," cried Andy (huh), "I'll fix you," as he attacked the Count (oil).

"Stop, stop," sobbed Sally (ahh).

"Stop, stop," cackled the Hag (cackle).

Meanwhile, the storm (boom) raged on, as all night the fight continued and the Atari machines shorted out.

By daybreak Andy (huh) and the Count (oil) were too tired to fight. Finally, the matter was settled.

The Count (oil) and the Hag (cackle) were married, moved to the oil well in Texas, and now star in their own sitcom entitled "Too Close for Comtrex."

Andy (huh) and Sally (ahh) were also married. Unfortunately, Andy (huh) found that Sally (ahh) only knew how to cook quiche.

Meanwhile, the storm (boom) lay in wait for the next Rose parade.

MAD LIBS SKIT: FIGHT OF THE CENTURY

Know how to play "Mad Libs"? This skit works the same way. When you introduce the skit, tell the audience that the script to the skit is not quite complete, and you need their help in finishing it. Then ask for the types of words indicated in the blanks in the script below. In other words, you might ask for a "noun," and the group should let their imaginations go and come up with the wildest noun they can think of. You write the words into the script. You don't tell the audience what the skit is about, of course. After the script is complete, the actors are chosen from the audience (choose kids who read well and can ham it up a bit—or you may want to choose some actors ahead of time and have them become familiar with their roles). Provide some simple costumes, and have your actors simply read their lines—expressively.

Characters:

The Announcer (with a microphone)
Cassius Cluck (dressed like a prizefighter with robe and boxing gloves)
Joe Freezer (dressed the same way)

Announcer: Welcome to ABC's "Wild World of _____." We're here tonight
(pl. noun)
covering the "Fight of the Century" between Cassius Cluck and Joe Freezer. As the crowd continues to file into beautiful Madison Square _____, we'll
(noun)
stop over here and have a few words with Joe and Cassius. Cassius, how do you predict the fight will go?

Cassius: I'll take him in the third _____.
(noun)

Joe: That's what you think, cause when I get through with you, you'll wish you were
_____.
(adj.)

Announcer: Joe, just how many _____ have you won by a knockout?
(plural noun)

Joe: _____. And this will be one more!
(number)

Cassius: You'll eat your _____, Freezer! When the _____ rings, I'm
(noun) (noun)
going to make you look like _____ out there. I'm going to ram my fist
(person)
down your _____.
(noun)

Joe:	Sticks and stones may break my bones, Cassius, but _____ will never (pl. noun) hurt me!
Announcer:	Fellas, how much money will you make on this fight?
Cassius:	I'll make two million _____. (pl. noun)
Joe:	Me too. With all that loot, I'm going to buy a _____ and move to (noun) _____. Then everyone will know that I am _____. (place) (adj.)
Cassius:	When I get through with you, Freezer, everyone will know that you are _____ and that I am the world heavyweight _____. (adj.) (noun)
Announcer:	Well, it's been great talking to you two _____. (pl. noun)

THE SEAGULL AND THE SURFER

Here is a great spontaneous skit that demands no props and no preparation. The "characters" can be chosen on the spot. Their instructions are simple. As the narrator reads the story slowly, each "character" is to act out what is being described. For example: "The waves rise in great swells" (the people who are "waves" begin to rise, then crouch, repeatedly). Be sure the narrator gives the "actors" enough time to do what is being described.

Characters:

Sun
Seagulls (any number)
Waves (any number)

Surfer
Shore (any number)

The Script: (read by the narrator)

It is a bright and beautiful morning at the beach. The *sun* is slowly rising, and the *seagulls* are waking up after a long night's rest; the waves are calm and serene and the *shore* is smooth and damp.

The ocean world now seems to come alive as the *seagulls* chatter to each other and fly off on their morning search for food. As the *gulls* fly over the *shore* and *waves*, they begin to get playful. They soar higher and higher, then drop suddenly, skimming the *waves* with their outstretched wings. They fly up, then up and down again, in circles, in zigzags, backwards, then forwards. The *gulls* are chattering noisily, screaming as loud as they can. Suddenly, the playfulness ends and the *gulls* return slowly to their nests to rest.

The *waves* are beginning to rise in great swells. They rise higher and higher reaching farther and farther until at the last second they come crashing down on each other and roll onto the *shore*.

A *surfer* arrives at the beach, walking on the *shore*. Excited at the prospect of the big *waves* that are continuing to break on the *shore*, the *surfer* begins to jump up and down. He sits on the *shore* and gazes at the breaking *waves*.

The *surfer* now decides to take his board out into the water. He paddles out, using fast, long strokes. He paddles faster and faster with longer and harder strokes until he reaches a point beyond the *waves*. Now, riding his board, he dodges skillfully in and out among the *waves* with precision timing. Poised and graceful, he "hangs ten" on his surfboard. Suddenly, a *wave* grabs him and sends him crashing into the *shore*.

The *surfer*, now tired and beaten, gathers up his surfboard and slowly stumbles away from the *shore* and heads for home.

The day is coming to an end as the *sun* slowly sets. The *gulls* make their last flight for the day flying over the *shore* and *waves* and once again return to their nests for a cozy night's sleep, tucking their wings under their bodies and lowering their heads.

As we take one last look at the beautiful ocean scene before the *sun* sets, we can see the restful *seagulls*, and the *waves* beating on the shore.

SPONTANEOUS MELODRAMAS

The following four skits are all done the same way. Characters are chosen from the audience and are asked to simply carry out the actions that are called for in the script. It's best to provide appropriately silly costumes for each player.

AS THE STOMACH TURNS

Characters:

Narrator
Lucille Lovelorn (best played by a guy)

Philip Pharpar (holding a picture frame in front of him)
Franklin Pharpar (with ring and phony check)
A door (a person standing using fist as doorknob)
A table (one or two people on their hands and knees)
A telephone (a person sitting on table using arm as receiver)

Props:

A ring
A phony check

The narration:

And now, the _____ present another episode in the continuing real-life drama, "As the Stomach Turns." Last time, luscious Lucille Lovelorn had spurned Dr. Preakbeak's advances because her precious Philip Pharpar would soon be graduating from law school and they would be married.

Today's scene opens with Lucille standing next to the picture of Philip which is hanging on the wall of her apartment.

Lucille is humming a happy tune to herself as she stares wistfully at her beloved Philip.

"Philip, I miss you so much," she says as she caresses his cheek. "Hurry home to me," she begs.

Then she kisses his picture passionately.

Suddenly, the telephone rings.

Lucille prances to the table, picks up the receiver, and sweetly says, "Hello—Oh, Gladys, it's you."

Then she frowns darkly.

Philip had found someone new. Philip had told Gladys to tell Lucille goodbye forever.

Lucille slams down the receiver angrily and begins to cry.

She runs over to the picture of Philip and screams, "You cad."

Then she slaps his picture viciously and begins to cry louder.

She takes the picture of Philip and turns it to the wall and begins to cry even louder.

Then she throws herself on the floor and begins to cry still louder.

Suddenly, Franklin Pharpar, Philip's younger brother, approaches the door and begins to knock vigorously.

Lucille gets up, straightens her hair and skirt, and jerks open the door.

Franklin enters the room quickly and says, "Lucille, have you been crying?"

"What's it to you, Batface?" pouts Lucille.

Then she slaps him painfully across the face.

Franklin slams the door as viciously as Lucille had slapped him.

"I'm sorry," cries Lucille.

Then she begins to weep upon his shoulder.

"Philip left me," she sobs as she points to the telephone.

"Tommyrot," says Franklin as he steps back quickly. "He does love you," he says.

"He sent me with this for you," he says.

Lucille gives a shriek of joy as she takes the ring from Franklin's hand.

Then she gives Franklin a big hug.

Lucille leaps to Philip's picture and spins it around to face her.

"I love you too, darling," she cooes.

Then she kisses his picture even more passionately than before.

Lucille begins dancing around the room with Franklin.

Suddenly, the telephone rings again.

Lucille hops to the phone and jerks up the receiver.

"Hello, hello, hello," she sings happily.

"Oh, Philip, it's you," she sighs.

But then a frown clouds her face.

He *has* found someone else; they *are* through.

She slams down the receiver and angrily throws the ring to the floor.

Then she whirls and slaps Franklin.

"You are a liar," she screams.

Then she jumps to Philip's picture.

"You are a worthless animal," she shrieks.

Then she slaps his picture mercilessly.

Then she wrenches the picture from the wall and throws it to the floor.

Franklin drops to one knee and clasps his hands.

"But I love you, my flower," he sings. "And I have something more valuable than a ring for you, my pet."

Then Franklin pulls a check from his pocket for the amount of _____.

Here is the supreme gift. He wants to pay her way to _____.
Lucille squeals with delight.
"What a lovely thought, darling," she sighs.
They embrace happily.
Then they walk over Philip's picture and out the door to their new life ahead.

A CHRISTMAS STORY

Cast:

Penelope Pureheart
Dirty Dan
Elmer Schmidlap
Faithful Dog Shep (a boy who gets down on all fours)
Christmas Tree (a boy or girl who holds his or her arms out)
Narrator

Props:

Chair
Tree decorations
Clean toilet brush

Story:

Our action takes place in the deep, snow-covered woods. Poor Penelope Pureheart is out with her faithful dog Shep, trying to find a Christmas tree for their poor, dreary hut. Penelope finds a pretty little tree . . . but . . . no . . . Shep's already found it.

After searching some more, she finds the perfect one! She chops it down, yells, "Timber!" and down it falls. She drags it back to her house with the help of her faithful dog Shep.

Now we see the poor, dreary hut. It looks so poor and dreary, except for the beautiful Christmas tree in the corner. She doesn't have any presents to go under it, but it is pretty anyway.

Suddenly, we hear a knock at the door. In bursts Dirty Dan. He demands that Poor Penelope

Pureheart pay him the $29.65 plus tax for the tree. She pleads with him to let her have it. Doesn't he know it is more blessed to give than to receive? "Bah, Humbug! I'll give you six hours or I'll take it back!" he says as he leaves.

Poor Penelope Pureheart doesn't know what to do. She has no money. She sits down on the chair and starts crying. Her faithful dog Shep comes over to comfort her. She pats him on the head. She scratches him under the chin. She rubs his ears. He loves it!

To comfort her, he licks her hand, then licks her arm all the way to the elbow. She loves it! It makes her feel so much better.

"What will we do?" she asks. "I wish Santa Claus would help us."

All of a sudden, there is a knock on the door. She knows it is Dirty Dan coming to get the money or her tree.

"Come in," she says sadly. But—instead of Dirty Dan—it is Elmer Schmidlap, former Fuller Brush salesman and now Santa Claus's vice president in charge of public relations. With him, he has his magic toilet brush, with which he performs various and sundry deeds of prestidigitation and other magical arts.

"What's wrong, Poor Penelope?" asks Elmer. She tells him and then breaks down crying. This goes on and on. Then her faithful dog Shep starts howling. This goes on and on.

At that moment, in bursts Dirty Dan. He demands the money or the tree.

Elmer says, "Can't you be nice, you dirty thing?"

Dan pushes Elmer and he falls into the beautiful Christmas tree.

"Now look what you've done," says Dirty Dan. "You've ruined the Christmas tree."

Elmer says, "We've had enough of your dirtiness, Dirty Dan. From now on you'll bring joy to the hearts of people." Then Elmer touches Dirty Dan with his magic toilet brush and Dirty Dan turns into the most beautiful Christmas tree there ever was!

Elmer and Penelope and Penelope's faithful dog Shep go out for a Christmas walk, celebrating with all of Santa's assistants. Dirty Dan just stands in the hut looking beautiful.

And thus our story ends.

Moral: If you get to the root of it all, all dirty, evil people are really saps.

DUDLEY DO-RIGHT

Characters:

The hero, Dudley Do-Right
The heroine, Prudence Pureheart
The villain, Dirty Dan
Grandmother
The dog (a boy who gets down on all fours)
The cat (a girl who does the same)
The chair (a boy on his hands and knees)
The table (two boys, side by side on their hands and knees)

As our story opens, we find ourselves in a densely wooded forest where lovely Prudence Pureheart is picking wild blackberries while whistling a merry tune. (Pause while Prudence whistles and picks.) Unbeknownst to her, the village villain, Dirty Dan, is creeping up behind her.

He grabs her and tries to steal a kiss!

She screams loud and long.

The villain covers her mouth with his hand as she screams.

She slaps the villain in the face.

He picks her up over his shoulder and carries her.

She screams and beats him.

He marches around in a circle three times, then heads for home to steal her Grandmother's money.

They exit.

Meanwhile, back at the ranch . . .

Prudence's grandmother is sitting on a chair stirring some cake batter on the table.

The cat is sleeping underneath the table.

The old dog, Shep, enters the house and barks at the cat.

The cat jumps into Grandma's lap.

Grandmother slaps the cat and says, "Get down, you dirty creature."

The cat jumps down and runs outside.

The dog comes over and licks Grandma's hand.

He keeps licking her hand all the way up to the elbow.

Grandma kicks the dog.

The dog goes and lies in the corner.

Just then, the villain enters the room with Prudence on his shoulder.

Grandmother screams.

The villain says, "I am taking Prudence and your money."

The dog rushes over and bites the villain on the leg.

The villain kicks the dog and lets Prudence down.

Prudence faints onto the floor.

The dog barks at the villain, then goes over and starts licking Prudence's face to revive her.

He licks her face for fifteen seconds while she remains perfectly still.

Just then, our hero, Dudley Do-Right, enters and shouts. "Forsooth and anon!"

Prudence stands up and screams, "Oh, my darling Dudley!"

Dudley and Prudence embrace.

Dudley says, "I love you, my precious."

Prudence says, "I love you, my little lotus blossom."

Suddenly, the villain picks up the chair and throws it at Dudley.

It knocks Dudley to the floor.

Prudence faints and falls onto the table.

Grandmother tries to revive her by slapping her hand, while sobbing, "My child, my child." This goes on and on . . .

The cat reenters the house, jumps on the chair, and runs underneath the table.

Dudley jumps up and begins flexing his muscles.

The villain begins to tremble and shake and his knees knock together. This goes on and on. The dog starts barking and the cat starts meowing and this goes on and on.

Dudley decides to warm up for the fight so he does a few exercises, starting out with ten jumping jacks. Then he runs in place for fifteen seconds.

All this time Grandmother is sobbing and slapping, the villain is trembling, the dog is barking, and the cat is meowing.

Then Dudley does fifteen pushups.

On the fifteenth pushup, the villain seizes his opportunity and hits Dudley on the head.

Dudley falls to the floor, unconscious.

Just then the cat scratches the dog's nose.

The dog and cat have a fight right on top of Dudley for ten seconds.

Then the dog chases the cat outside. Just then the table collapses under Prudence's weight and falls to the ground . . . table, Prudence, Grandmother, and all.

Prudence remains unconscious.

Granny shouts, "You nasty villain!" and starts hitting him in the stomach.

The villain doubles over.

Granny then goes around and kicks him in the seat.

The villain straightens up.

She hits him in the stomach over and over.

The villain again bends over.

She gives him a rabbit punch on the back of the neck.

He collapses unconscious to the floor.

Granny looks around at the three unconscious bodies.

She then straightens her shawl around her head and goes out the door for a night on the town, saying, "All's well that ends well!"

PUDDLES, THE WONDER DOG

Characters:

Robust Ronnie, the hero
Bashful Bo, the heroine
Naughty Nixon, the villain
Puddles, the wonder dog
The babbling brook, two people lying down
The trees, two people standing with arms outstretched
The mirror, a person standing upright
The train, three people in a row

Scene One: (read by the narrator)

Our scene opens as Bashful Bo is looking through the forest for her lost poodle, Puddles. In the background, she hears the swaying of the trees (the trees sway), the babbling of the brook (the brook babbles), and the croaking of the frogs (the audience.)

But in the nearby shadows, closely behind a tree . . . I said CLOSELY behind a tree . . . the evil villain Naughty Nixon lurks cautiously. He sneaks up behind Bo to steal a kiss. Bashful Bo, startled by the attempt, screams . . . with vibrato . . . then faints.

Puddles, who has been hiding behind a tree, living up to his name . . . sees what has transpired and comes to the rescue just as Naughty Nixon attempts to kidnap the fainted Bashful Bo.

Puddles runs up to Naughty Nixon, sticks his tongue out, bites Nixon's leg, then does a Nixon victory impersonation. Naughty Nixon picks up Puddles, and throws him into the babbling brook. The brook shields . . . I said the *Brooke Shields* . . . itself by making waves.

Then, Naughty Nixon jumps into the brook and tries to drown Puddles. The scene is desperate. Puddles gasps for air and then burps. Naughty Nixon shouts, "No one can do a terrible impersonation of me like that and get away with it. Besides, I'm not a crook. I didn't erase the tapes!" Somehow Puddles escapes.

Naughty Nixon gets out of the brook, shakes off his wet shoes, and returns to pick up and steal away Bashful Bo. He exits. Puddles scampers off to call the hero Robust Ronnie.

Scene Two:

Scene two opens with Robust Ronnie looking into a full-length mirror, singing a made-up song with the only words "Ain't I something," to the tune of "Three Blind Mice."

He combs his freshly dyed hair, puts in his dentures, then gets a rear-view look at his Calvin Kleins. He opens his mouth wide to check his teeth. He gets closer to the mirror to remove a zit from his face. He flexes. Then he does a series of exercises. He jogs in place. He does five jumping jacks.

Puddles runs in, barking, and tries to explain what has happened to Bashful Bo. Since he doesn't speak, he stands on his hind legs to imitate Bo's walk, so our hero will know who he's talking about. Robust Ronnie, because of age, still looks confused about who Puddles is trying to impersonate. Puddles continues by describing Bo's figure in dog and sign language. "Well, I think you're talking about Bo," answers Ronnie.

Scene Three:

Meanwhile, Naughty Nixon is tying Bashful Bo to the railroad tracks, because she never gave him a kiss. He makes one last attempt and she slaps him silly.

So he finishes tying her up on the tracks. Far away, in the distance, the train is heard. Bo shivers.

Robust Ronnie and Puddles enter. Ronnie grabs Nixon, twirls him around and gives him a punch in the belly. The train gets closer. Naughty Nixon tells Robust Ronnie to look up to see the Goodyear Blimp. Ronnie obliges, and receives a punch in the belly. Ronnie backs up. Now he's mad. He does a series of karate moves. Naughty Nixon punches Ronnie and knocks him out.

Meanwhile, Puddles has untied the rope from Bo and saves her in the nick of time. Puddles then attacks Naughty Nixon with a punch in the belly—with his head. Afraid of the angry dog, Naughty Nixon tries to convince everyone that he's innocent of any wrongdoing to Bo. He gives the "who me?" look.

This doesn't fool Puddles. He barks out "enough" in dog language and knocks out Naughty Nixon with a spinning judo chop he had just learned in his aerobic judo and Chinese cooking class. Bo faints, again.

Puddles looks over the scene and realizes—yes, this old dog can learn new tricks.

WILD WEST SHOW

This can be done one of two ways: either select seven kids to come to the front and each take one of the parts below, or have the entire group get into seven smaller groups, with each group taking one of the parts. Each part requires no acting, only sound effects. The person (or group) assigned to each part simply makes the appropriate sound effect each time their part's name comes up in the story, which is read by a narrator. The parts and corresponding sound effects are:

The cowboys ("Whoopee!")
The Indians (an Indian yell with war dance)
The women (scream)
The horses (clippety-clop with hands and feet)
The stagecoach ("Rumble, rumble," make circular motions with arms, like wheels)
The rifles ("Bang, bang!")
The bows and arrows ("Zip, zip," do the motions with hands)

The characters (or the groups) should try to overdo their parts and outdo each other. Every time one of the parts comes up in the story, the narrator should pause and allow time for the sound effect or motion. Give the winner (the person or group who does the best job) a prize.

The Story:

It was in the days of *stagecoaches* and *cowboys* and *Indians*. Alkali Ike, Dippy Dick, and Pony Pete were three courageous *cowboys*. When the *stagecoach* left for Rainbow's End they were aboard, as were also two *women*, Salty Sal and a doll-faced blonde. The *stagecoach* was drawn by three handsome *horses* and it left Dead End exactly on time.

The most dangerous part of the journey was the pass known as Gory Gulch. As the *stagecoach* neared this spot, the *women* were a bit nervous and the *cowboys* were alert, fingering their *rifles* as if to be ready for any emergency. Even the *horses* seemed to sense the danger.

Sure enough—just as the *stagecoach* entered the Gulch, there sounded the blood-curdling war cry of the *Indians*. Mounted on *horses,* they rode wildly toward the *stagecoach* aiming their *bows and arrows*. The *cowboys* took aim with their *rifles* and fired. The *women* screamed. The *horses* pranced nervously. The *Indians* shot their *bows and arrows*. The *cowboys* aimed their *rifles* again, this time shooting with more deadly effect. The leading brave fell and the *Indians* turned their *horses* and fled, leaving their *bows and arrows* behind. The *women* fainted. The *cowboys* shot one more volley from their *rifles* just for luck. The driver urged on the *horses* and the *stagecoach* sped down the trail.

CHAPTER SEVEN

GROANERS, QUICKIES AND ONE-LINERS

BORIS AND HORACE

Here's a skit for two people that is basically a collection of one-line gags, fat and skinny jokes, and insults.

Boris: Hey, how you doin', Horace? You're looking great!

Horace: Thanks, Boris. Good to see you again.

Boris: We've sure had some good times together, haven't we?

Horace: We sure have!

Boris: Hey, do you remember that funny couple from our old neighborhood—the Glickenheimers?

Horace: You mean the guy whose wife was hurt while taking a milk bath. The cow slipped and fell on her, right?

Boris: Yeah, that's the one. Her face looked like it wore out six bodies!

Horace: She had such a sour look that when she put on face cream, it would curdle!

Boris: Yeah, she made him a millionaire. Of course, before they were married he was a MULTI-millionaire.

Horace: She couldn't cook or clean house, but boy she could lick her weight in trading stamps!

Boris: As I remember, she was real thin. If it weren't for her adam's apple, she wouldn't have any figure at all!

Horace: She recently swallowed an olive and was rushed to the maternity ward!

Boris: It takes *two* of her to make a shadow!

Horace: The only way she could get any color in her face was to stick out her tongue!

Boris: If she ever got a run in her nylons, she'd fall out!

Horace: She'd be so tired at the end of the day she could hardly keep her mouth open!

Boris: She was so thin that when her husband would take her to the restaurant, the head waiter would ask him to check his umbrella!

Horace: Yeah, she had to run around in the shower to get wet!

Boris: She would have to wear skis in the shower to keep from going down the drain!

Horace: If she stood sideways and stuck out her tongue, she looked just like a zipper!

Boris:	Her husband made a movie that no one liked. In fact, I have seen better film on teeth! I have seen more excitement at an opening of an umbrella!
Horace:	Yeah, the entire audience was hissing at him, except for one man. He was applauding the hissing!
Boris:	The only thing he ever achieved on his own is dandruff!
Horace:	He left his first job because of fatigue—his boss was tired of him.
Boris:	The only reason he manages to keep his head above water is that wood floats!
Horace:	His psychiatrist told him that he didn't have an inferiority complex. He's just inferior, period.
Boris:	He's the real decisive type. He'll always give you a definite "maybe."
Horace:	He's so nervous he keeps coffee awake.
Boris:	They call him "Jigsaw" for short. That's because he keeps falling apart.
Horace:	He's skinny, too. His muscles look like flea bites on spaghetti!
Boris:	After they made him, they must have broken the jelly mold.
Horace:	Yeah, they call him the "Rock of Jello!"
Boris:	Before he was married, he sent his picture to the "lonely hearts club." They replied that they weren't *that* lonely!
Horace:	He now carries pictures of his children and a sound track of his wife.
Boris:	He's always catching something. Why, he won't even talk on the phone to anyone who is sick.
Horace:	He's so full of penicillin, every time he sneezes, he cures thirty people.
Boris:	I heard that he stopped drinking coffee in the morning because it keeps him awake during the day.
Horace:	He's the kind of guy you ask to stick around if you want to be alone.
Boris:	Somebody told me the other day he was hit by a hit-and-run driver . . .
Horace:	Yeah, when the traffic cop asked him if he got the number of the license plate, he said "No, but I'd recognize my wife's laugh anywhere!"
Boris:	Well, I've got to go now, Horace. See you later.
Horace:	Take it easy, Boris! Next time!

CARRYING A CASE TO COURT

These are four short sequences that should all be done in the same meeting, but not one right after the other. Space them so that the "guy" in the sequences interrupts unexpectedly several times during the meeting.

1. The guy enters the room carrying a case of pop bottles. The M.C. asks, "Hey, where are you going with that?" The guy answers, "Oh, I'm just taking a case to court."

2. The guy enters a second time, carrying a case and a ladder. The M.C. asks, "Where are you going NOW?" The guy replies, "Oh, I'm taking my case to a higher court."

3. The guy enters again, this time with a girl. The M.C. asks, "What's going on here?" The guy says, "I'm just going to court."

4. Once more, the guy enters, this time with only his underwear on. The M.C. says, "Hey, you can't come in here like this! Where are you going?" He answers, "I lost my suit."

THE DREAM

This is a skit for two guys.

Person #1: Last night I dreamed that I went to heaven.

Person #2: Oh, really? What was it like?

Person #1: Well, as I was walking up to the pearly gates, I felt something tugging on my arm. I looked around and there was an *old ugly woman* chained to my wrist. I tried to get her off, but I couldn't. She was chained on there for good!

Person #2: Sounds more like a nightmare to me! What did you do?

Person #1: I saw Saint Peter standing there at the gate, so I asked him why that old woman was chained to my wrist.

Person #2: What did he say?

Person #1: He said that I had lived a pretty rotten life while I was on earth, and that that old woman was the "burden" that I was going to have to bear with me throughout eternity in order to pay for all the rotten things I had done. I was just stuck with her.

Person #2: Why, that's terrible. But at least you were in heaven.

Person #1: That's the way I decided to look at it. So, I went on into heaven, just dragging my burden along behind me. And guess what? While I was walking along those streets of gold, I saw *you* up in heaven too.

Person #2: *I* was in your dream?

Person #1: You sure were. And *you* had a woman chained to your wrist, too!

Person #2: Oh, no!

Person #1: But she wasn't ugly. She was young and beautiful!

Person #2: *(smiling)* I had a *beautiful* girl chained to my wrist? Hey, I think I like your dream after all!

Person #1: I didn't think it was fair, so I went over and asked St. Peter why *I* had an old ugly woman chained to my wrist, while *you* had a pretty girl chained to *your* wrist.

Person #2: So what did he say? *(smiling)*

Person #1: He said, "Well—that's because that pretty girl lived a pretty rotten life, too!"

FLAT TIRE

The scene for this short skit is a roadside. A woman is trying to change her flat tire, but is obviously having a difficult time. A gentleman happens along and offers to help.

He: What seems to be the problem?

She: I have a flat tire and I don't know how to work this crazy thing. *(She points to the jack.)*

He: Maybe I can help. By the way, how did you get the flat?

She: I was in such a hurry that I ran over a milk bottle.

He: Didn't you see it?

She: How could I? The dumb little kid had it in his pocket.

GROANERS

These skits are short "one-liners" that can be used in many different ways. In some cases, the "punch line" is funny enough to carry the skit, but in most cases, the real humor is in the acting out of the skit by the participants. Timing and execution are important in skits like these.

One good way to use these skits is to select a number of them (twenty or so) and present them all at once "shotgun" style—one right after another. There should be no pause between them at all. Have the necessary props out on the stage ahead of time for all the skits, and encourage the kids to act their parts with gusto. You can use just a few kids, if you'd like, and have them switch costumes back and forth, acting out many different parts. It helps, too, to have a lively musical interlude between each skit, such as old time piano music or a vaudeville-type fanfare. Use your imagination and creativity and the result will be a lot of fun for everyone.

THE HOLDUP

Man: Say, buddy, do you see any cops around?

Stranger: No.

Man: O.K., then—stick-em-up!

THE BEAUTY SHOP

Smith: My wife spent four hours in the beauty shop this morning!
Jones: That's a long time.
Smith: You're not kidding. And that was just for the estimate!

THE HAT

Lady: My husband says I look younger in this hat.
Friend: Oh, really? How old are you?
Lady: Thirty.
Friend: No, I mean, without the hat. . . .

THE DREAM

Wife: Dear, I dreamed you gave me a hundred dollars for new clothes last night.
            You wouldn't want to spoil that nice dream, now, would you?
Husband: Of course not, dear. You can keep the money.

THE SANDWICH SHOP

Customer: Waiter, the sign outside says that you'll pay fifty dollars to anyone who can
            order a sandwich that you don't have. O.K., I'd like an *elephant ear*
            sandwich!

Waiter:	Uh-oh. Guess we'll have to pay you the fifty bucks.
Customer:	No elephants ears, eh? (smiling)
Waiter:	Nah, we've got lots of them. We're just out of those big buns.

AT THE DOOR

Visitor:	Was that your wife who met me at the door and took my hat and coat?
Man:	You don't think I'd hire a maid that ugly, do you?

THE HANGMAN

Hangman:	(as he places the noose around the criminal's neck) You'll have to excuse me if I seem a little nervous. You see, this is my first hanging.
Criminal:	Mine, too.

THE ROPE

Observer:	Say, what are you pulling that rope for?
Man:	Have you ever tried to push one of these things?

THE WIRE

Messenger:	Wire for Mr. Jones! Wire for Mr. Jones!
Jones:	I'm Mr. Jones.
Messenger:	Here you are, sir. (Hands him a piece of wire.)

THE ESKIMOS

One Eskimo:	I saw someone kissing your wife last night.
Other Eskimo:	Yeah, well, that's no skin off my nose.

THE REVEREND AND THE GOLF BALL

Man:	Reverend, I'm really sorry that I swore like that. That's what I like about you. When your ball goes in the rough you never swear.
Reverend:	That may be . . . but when I spit, the grass dies!

THE MEDICINE

Lady:	The doctor told me to drink this medicine after a hot bath.
Friend:	Did you drink it?
Lady:	No. I could hardly finish drinking the hot bath.

THE MIND READER

Mind reader:	Would you like your palm read?
Customer:	Yes.
Mind reader:	*(Takes out red paint, and paints his hand.)*

ON THE AIRLINER

Stewardess:	Sir, I think we left your wife behind in Chicago!
Man:	Oh, thank goodness. I thought I was going deaf.

THE COED

Girl:	I went away to college to find Mr. Perfect, but when I got there I found out I wasn't the only pebble on the beach.

| *Friend:* | What did you do? |
| *Girl:* | I became a little boulder. |

THE TIE

Man:	Say, that's a beautiful rainbow tie you're wearing.
Other man:	What do you mean, *rainbow* tie?
Man:	It has a big *pot* at the end.

THE BUS RIDE

Lady:	Sir, are you enjoying your bus ride?
Man:	Yes, ma'am.
Lady:	Then why are you sitting there with your eyes shut? Are you sick?
Man:	No, I'm O.K. It's just that I hate to see a woman stand.

HAND-ME-DOWNS

Smith:	We were so poor when I was a kid that I had to wear "hand-me-downs"!
Jones:	That's not so bad. Everybody has to wear hand-me-downs.
Smith:	But all I had were older sisters!

THE SINGER

Singer:	(*using a strainer for a microphone*) "Somewhere . . . over the rainbow . . .
Man:	Hey, don't do that!
Singer:	(*Stops singing.*) Why?
Man:	You'll strain your voice.

THE POOR MAN

Poor man:	My family was really poor.
Friend:	How do you know they were so poor?
Poor man:	That's easy. Every time I passed someone in town, they would say, "There goes Bobby Jones. His *poor* family . . ."

UGLY BABY

Passenger: Lady, that is the ugliest baby I've ever seen!
Lady: *(Starts crying.)*
Busdriver: *(Stops bus.)* What's the problem, ma'am? Here, use my handkerchief—and here's a banana for your monkey.

THE GALLOWS

Man: Hey, what are you guys doing!
Bully: We're hanging this man! In this town, we hang all murderers and all sissies!
Man: *(in a real deep voice)* Oh, really?

IN THE OFFICE

Employee: Say, boss, since your assistant died, I was wondering if maybe I could take his place.
Employer: It's all right with me if you can arrange it with the undertaker.

THE PASTOR

Member: Pastor, how did you get that cut on your face?
Pastor: I was thinking about my sermon this morning, and wasn't concentrating on what I was doing—and I cut myself shaving.
Member: That's too bad. Next time, you'd better concentrate on your shaving and cut your sermon!

THE NEW HAT

Husband: Where did you get that new hat?
Wife: Don't worry, dear. It didn't cost a thing. It was marked down from $20 to $10. So I bought it with the $10 that I saved.

CROSSED UP

Smith: Know what they got when they crossed an abalone with a crocodile?

Jones:	No, what?
Smith:	A "Crock-a-baloney."

THE FRESH GUY

Girl:	When I went out with Pete, I had to slap his face five times.
Friend:	Was he that fresh?
Girl:	No. I thought he was dead.

THE TEACHER

Girl:	Did you kiss me when the lights went out?
Boy:	No!
Girl:	It must have been that guy over there.
Boy:	Oh, yeah? I'll teach him a thing or two!
Girl:	You couldn't teach him a thing!

THE PIE

Man:	Waitress, what kind of pie is this that I'm eating?
Waitress:	Well, what does it taste like?
Man:	It tastes like fish.
Waitress:	Oh, that must be the lemon pie. The apple pie tastes like garlic.

THE PIZZA

Cook:	Say, mister. Do you want me to cut this pizza into six pieces, or eight?
Man:	You better make it six. I don't think I can eat eight.

THE GORILLA

Smith:	Know what they got when they crossed a gorilla with a porcupine?
Jones:	No, what?
Smith:	I don't know what they call it, but it sure gets a seat on the subway.

WHALE SANDWICH

Man: Say, waiter. Your sign outside says, "Any sandwich you can name." O.K. I want a *whale* sandwich!

Waiter: One whale sandwich coming up. *(Leaves, goes into kitchen, and comes out again.)* Sorry. I can't get you a whale sandwich.

Man: Why not? Your sign says, "Any sandwich!"

Waiter: Well, the cook says he doesn't want to start a new whale for one lousy sandwich.

THE SERVICE

Man: Isn't this a beautiful church? Look . . . here's a plaque on the wall dedicated to all the brave men who died in the service.

Lady: Which one . . . morning or evening?

MOUNTAIN LION

Smith: Know what they got when they crossed a mountain lion and a parrot?

Jones: No, what?

Smith: I don't know what they call it, but when it talks, you listen!

BULLFIGHTER

Man: Did you hear about the bullfighter who became a fireman?

Other man: No. What about him?

Man: Well, he went to a fire and some guy jumped out of a three-story window into his net.

Other man: Then what happened?

Man: He went, "Ole!" *(Moves net like in bullfight.)*

SNAKE BITE

Smith: Know what they got when they crossed a rattlesnake with a horse?

Jones: No, what?

Smith: I don't know what they call it, but if it bites you, you can ride it to the hospital.

FLOWER DISEASE

Girl: He's got the horrible "flower disease"!
Other girl: What's that?
Girl: He's a blooming idiot!

THE CANARY

Man: Know what the 500-pound canary said?
Other man: No, what?
Man: (deep voice) CHIRP!

THE BANQUET

Speaker: This is terrible. I'm the speaker at this banquet and I forgot to bring my false teeth with me.
Man: I happen to have an extra pair. Try these.
Speaker: Too small.
Man: Well, try this pair.
Speaker: Too big.
Man: Well, I have one more pair . . . how about these?
Speaker: These fit just fine. Boy, I sure am lucky to be sitting next to a dentist.
Man: Oh, I'm not a dentist. I'm a mortician.

DIET SHAMPOO

Girl: Have you tried that new diet shampoo?
Boy: No.
Girl: Well, you should. It's for fatheads.

CHRISTMAS GIFT

Smith: What did you give your wife for Christmas last year?
Jones: A cemetery plot.
Smith: What are you going to give her this year?
Jones: Nothing. She didn't use last year's gift.

THE GET-WELL CARD

Man: How are you feeling, pastor?
Pastor: Much better, thank you.
Man: Well, we had a committee meeting the other night and they voted to send you this get-well card. The motion passed four to three.

DON'T WORRY

Man: You shouldn't worry like that. It doesn't do any good.
Other man: It does for me! Ninety percent of the things that I worry about never happen!

THE NIBBLE

Old lady: Dear, when we were younger, you used to nibble on my ear.
Old man: I'll be right back.
Old lady: Where are you going?
Old man: To get my teeth!

THE THREE WIVES

Man: Did you hear about the guy who had three wives in three months? The first two died from eating poison mushrooms.
Friend: What happened to the third?
Man: She died from a blow on the head. She wouldn't eat the mushrooms.

THE COMPUTER

Inventor: I've invented a computer that's almost human!

Man:	You mean it can think on its own?
Inventor:	No. But when it makes a mistake, it blames another computer!

THE DRESS

Woman:	This dress that I have on will never go out of style.
Other woman:	You're right. It'll look just as ridiculous every year.

ELEPHANT PAJAMAS

Hunter:	One night in the jungle, I heard a noise outside my tent. I looked outside and an elephant was charging. I ran outside, grabbed my gun, and shot him *in my pajamas!*
Man:	That's ridiculous. How did he ever get into your pajamas?

FAMOUS MEN

Visitor:	Have any famous men ever been born in this town?
Native:	Nope. Just little babies.

EVERY TWENTY MINUTES

Man:	According to this report, a person is hit by an automobile every twenty minutes!
Other man:	What a glutton for punishment that guy must be!

WANT AD

Girl:	My dog ran away last night.
Boy:	Did you put an ad in the paper?
Girl:	No.
Boy:	Why not?
Girl:	My dog can't read.

MUD PACKS

Man: Every so often, my wife puts on one of those mud packs.
Friend: Does it improve her looks?
Man: Yes, for a few days. Then the mud falls off.

THE OCEAN

Girl: You remind me of an ocean . . .
Boy: You mean—wild? Restless? Romantic?
Girl: No. I mean you make me sick.

THE NEWSBOY

Newsboy: Extra! Extra! Read all about it! Two men swindled!
Man: I'll take one. (Looks at paper.) Hey, there's nothing here about two men being swindled!
Newsboy: Extra! Extra! Three men swindled!

THE INHERITANCE

Girl: I think you only married me because my father left me a lot of money!
Husband: That's not true. I couldn't care less who left you the money!

HAVE YOU SEEN JOHN?

Here's a quickie that can get very confusing to an audience. There is a subtle shift in the dialogue that causes the first person to actually answer his own question.

Person #1:   Have you seen John?
Person #2:   What's his name?
Person #1:   Who?
Person #2:   John.
Person #1:   No, I haven't seen him.

HOT DOG

This skit uses just one actor, talking on the telephone. The audience, of course, hears only one side of the conversation. The only props needed are a play telephone and Tastee Freeze outfit.

Hello! This is Richard's Tastee Freeze.

Yes, we had an ad in the paper for dogs for sale.

Well, we have some a foot long and some smaller.

They came Wednesday. So they've been here about four days.

Oh, yes, they all came at the same time.

What? You thought the larger ones came first?

What color? They're all red.

Yes. We have some ready for Christmas. You want what? One for Judy, one for Jimmy, and one for Joey. Whatever you say.

What was that about them being broken?

No, lady, the ones that are broken, we don't sell.

What do we do to keep the drippings off the floor?

We wrap them in a napkin.

Right now they're back here in a box.

I guess there are about fifty in a box.

Yes, ma'am, it is kinda crowded.

Do we have paper under them? Yes, there is paper under each row.

No, ma'am, we don't take the paper out until we sell them. What did you say? I should be reported?

45¢ small and 75¢ foot long.

Yes, we think that is a good price too.

Registered? No, ma'am, but they have been inspected.

Yes, we think that is just as good, too.

Look, lady, I'm talking about *hot* dogs.

You don't care about their temperature?

Hair? Lady, our dogs do not have hair on them. Yes, I said no hair.

No, they will not grow any later. I told you these . . .

You don't want any sick dogs? You think they are sick because of their high temperature?

Lady! These are hot dogs! Hot dogs! HOT DOGS!
Yeah, well, same to you! *(Hangs up.)*

I'M NOT HERE

This short skit requires two people. Lines should be memorized and rehearsed. Timing is very important.

Person #1:   I'll bet you ten dollars that I'm not here.

Person #2:   Well, of course, you're here. Anyone can see that you are definitely here.

Person #1:   I'm telling you, I'm not here, and I'm going to prove to you that I'm not here.

Person #2:   O.K., you got yourself a bet.

Person #1:   Am I in Chicago right now?

Person #2:   Of course not.

Person #1:   Am I in New York City right now?

Person #2:   Don't be ridiculous.

Person #1:   O.K., if I'm not in Chicago, and I'm not in New York City, then I must be somewhere else, right?

Person #2:   Uh—right.

Person #1:   And if I'm "somewhere else," then—I can't be *here*, right?

Person #2:   Well, that does make sense *(looking puzzled).*

Person #1:   So, that proves that I'm not here, and you owe me ten bucks!

Person #2:   Hmmm. *(Starts to pull out wallet.)* I sure thought that was a safe bet. *(Person #1 holds out his hand, waiting to receive the money.)* Wait a minute! I can't pay you ten bucks!

Person #1:   Why not?

Person #2:   Because *you're not here!*

LEAVING HOME

A man sits in a chair reading a newspaper. A woman enters with a coat on and carrying a suitcase. She is apparently very upset. The man in the chair couldn't care less.

Woman: I've had it! I'm through! I'm leaving this crummy rotten house and all these crummy kids and going home to mother! I'm sick and tired of ironing, mopping, and cleaning up after you day in and day out! I tell you, I've had it! No more! I'm leaving and don't ask me to come back because I am leaving for good! *(sobbing)* Good bye! *(Stomps out of the room.)*

Man: *(Turns to an offstage room and yells.)* Alice, dear! The maid just quit.

MONK MONOTONY

This skit is for three people: the Main Monk, Monk Monotony, and the sign carrier. You will need one sign that reads "Ten Years Later." The scene is in a monastery where Monk Monotony has taken a vow of silence.

Main Monk: So, Monk Monotony, you have just taken a vow of silence? *(Monk Monotony nods head.)* Do you know what this vow of silence means? *(Monk Monotony nods head.)* That's right. You may not speak for ten years—and even then you may say only two words. You may go now.

(Monk Monotony exits. After about 20 seconds in which the Main Monk does nothing, the sign carrier enters slowly from right and exits slowly to the left, carrying the sign which reads "Ten Years Later." Monk Monotony enters.)

Main Monk: Well, Monk Monotony, your first ten years are up, and you may now say your two words.

Monk Monotony: Hard bed.

Main Monk: You may go now.

(Monk Monotony exits. After about 20 seconds in which the Main Monk does nothing, the sign carrier enters slowly from right and exits slowly to the left, carrying the sign that reads "Ten Years Later." Monk Monotony enters.)

Main Monk:	Well, Monk Monotony, your second ten years are up, and you may now say your two words.
Monk Monotony:	Bad food.
Main Monk:	You may go now.

(Monk Monotony exits. After about 20 seconds in which the Main Monk does nothing, the sign carrier enters slowly from right and exits slowly to the left, carrying the sign that reads "Ten Years Later." Monk Monotony enters.)

Main Monk:	Well, Monk Monotony, your third ten years are up, and you may now say your two words.
Monk Monotony:	I quit. *(He begins to exit immediately.)*
Main Monk:	*(to Monk Monotony as he is leaving)* Well, I am not surprised. You've been complaining ever since you got here.

THE NEWLYWEDS

The scene is the breakfast table of a newly married couple. For extra laughs, have both of the characters be guys, one dressed like a girl.

She:	Darling?
He:	Yes, dear?
She:	Isn't it wonderful being married?
He:	Sure is, sweetheart.
She:	Honey, I was just wondering something . . .
He:	Yes, sugarplum, what's that?
She:	Well, seeing as how we've been married only a few short hours and everything, I was just wondering if, before breakfast, you would come over here and give me a little kiss on the cheek . . . *(giggle)*
He:	*(embarrassed)* In broad daylight? Aw, gee . . .
She:	Please? Just a little peck on the cheek right here? *(Points to a place on her cheek.)*
He:	Welllll . . . O.K. *(He kisses her on the cheek.)*

She: Ahhhhh. Good! I've been trying to pop that zit for a week!

PASSED YOUR HOUSE THE OTHER DAY

Here's a quickie skit for two people:

Person #1:   Hey, I passed your house the other day!
Person #2:   How did you know it was my house?
Person #1:   I saw you out in the front yard.
Person #2:   Well, why didn't you wave or something?
Person #1:   I didn't recognize you.

QUICKIES

The idea behind each of these is the same. A guy comes running into the room acting strange, and the leader responds. It is best to have the guy come in at a seemingly inappropriate time, such as interrupting you as you are making an announcement. Most of these will get groans rather than wild laughter, so be prepared.

1. It's running down my back! It's running down my back!
   What is?
   My spine.
2. It's all around me! It's all around me!
   What is?
   My belt.
3. I can't see! I can't see!
   Why not?
   My eyes are closed.
4. It's all over us! It's all over us!
   What is?
   The roof.

5. Woman the lifeboats! We're sinking! Woman the lifeboats!
   Wait—you mean "man" the lifeboats, don't you?
   Look, you fill your lifeboats, I'll fill mine.
6. (Guy walks in carrying a paper bag.)
   What's in the bag?
   Milk.
   That's ridiculous. You don't put milk in a *bag*.
   Why not? Cows do.

SOME DO

This simple skit involves a guy, a girl, and a park bench. It begins with the two of them strolling onstage, toward the bench.

He: (nervously) Some night.
She: Yeah, some night.
He: Some moon.
She: Yeah, some moon.
He: Some stars.
She: Yeah, some stars. (They sit down on the bench.)
He: Some park.
She: Yeah, some park.
He: (Moves closer to her, then, using his fingers, notices dew on the bench.) Some dew.
She: Well, I DON'T! (She slaps him across the face, knocking him off the bench.)

THREE AGAINST A THOUSAND

Three guys walk in all bandaged up, smeared with dirt and blood, limping, moaning, and shaking their heads in disbelief over the fantastic battle they just went through. "What a battle, what fantastic odds! We should never have attempted it in the first place. Three guys against a thousand! Unbelievable!" Finally one guy says, "Yeah, they were the toughest three guys I've ever seen."

WILL SHE OR WON'T SHE?

Here's a short skit that is good for promoting a coming event that costs money or where dates are encouraged.

Guy: Will she or won't she? Will she or won't she?
Girl: *(walking by)* Will she or won't she what?
Guy: Will she or won't she go with me to the _____ ?
Girl: Who is "she"?
Guy: You.
Girl: Oh, I'd love to!
Guy: Will she or won't she? Will she or won't she?
Girl: What's the matter? I already told you that I'd go with you.
Guy: Will she or won't she buy her own ticket?
Girl: *(Slaps guy and chases him offstage.)*

YOU GOT ME BUDDY!

Scene: Two guys are sitting at a table in a restaurant, one reading a newspaper, so that you don't see his face. Another man dressed like a gangster enters the room and yells at the guy who is *not* reading the newspaper (from a distance).

Gangster: All right, Butch! I got you at last! You been running from me too long, and now I'm gonna finish you off!
Butch: Please, Big Al, I'll pay you back the dough I owe ya!
Gangster: Sorry, Butch, but you've had your last chance! *(Shoots him several times with a blank gun.)*
Butch: Ahhhhhggg! You got me pal! You got me buddy! *(yelling)* You got me pal!
Gangster: Well, then, fall down and die already.
Butch: But you didn't get me—you got me *pal. (Points to guy reading the newspaper, who suddenly falls over dead.)*